D1164071

The Price of the Euro

The Price of the Euro

Edited by

Jonas Ljungberg
Department of Economic History
Lund University, Sweden

First published 2004 by
PALGRAVE MACMILLAN
Houndmills, Basingstoke, Hampshire RG21 6XS and
175 Fifth Avenue, New York, N.Y. 10010
Companies and representatives throughout the world

PALGRAVE MACMILLAN is the global academic imprint of the Palgrave
Macmillan division of St. Martin's Press, LLC and of Palgrave Macmillan Ltd.
Macmillan® is a registered trademark in the United States, United Kingdom
and other countries. Palgrave is a registered trademark in the European
Union and other countries.

ISBN 1–4039–3497–5

This book is printed on paper suitable for recycling and made from fully
managed and sustained forest sources.

A catalogue record for this book is available from the British Library.

Library of Congress Cataloging-in-Publication Data
Eurons pris. English.
  The price of the Euro / edited by Jonas Ljungberg.
    p. cm.
  Includes bibliographical references and index.
  ISBN 1–4039–3497–5 (cloth)
  1. Euro. 2. Economic and Monetary Union. 3. Monetary union—
European Union countries. 4. Monetary union—Sweden. 5. Europe—
Economic integration. I. Ljungberg, Jonas. II. Title.
  HG925.E873913 2004
  332.4′94—dc22   2004043619

10   9   8   7   6   5   4   3   2   1
13   12   11   10   09   08   07   06   05   04

Printed and bound in Great Britain by
Antony Rowe Ltd, Chippenham and Eastbourne

Contents

List of Tables

List of Figures

Notes on the Contributors

James Forder is Lecturer in Economics at Balliol College, Oxford University, United Kingdom.

James Foreman-Peck is Professor of Economics and Director of the Welsh Institute for Research in Economics and Development at Cardiff Business School, United Kingdom.

Jesper Jespersen is Professor of Economics at Roskilde University, Denmark.

Arjo Klamer is Professor of Cultural Economics at Erasmus University Rotterdam, The Netherlands.

Hans Albin Larsson is Professor of History at the School of Education and Communication, Jönköping University, Sweden.

Jonas Ljungberg is Associate Professor of Economic History at Lund University, Sweden.

Renate Ohr is Professor of Economics at the Georg-August University of Göttingen, Germany.

Roland Vaubel is Professor of Economics at the University of Mannheim, Germany.

Preface

A Swedish edition of this volume appeared three weeks before 14 September 2003, when a majority of the electorate in Sweden voted 'No' to replace the krona with the euro. 'No' received 56 per cent and 'Yes' 42 per cent of the 83 per cent of the electorate participating in the referendum. The majority against the euro, 14 percentage points, was so large that the rejection echoed far beyond the borders of Sweden.

Interestingly, four parties with 280 of the 349 seats in the parliament campaigned for the euro. Three parties with only a fifth of the seats campaigned for the defence of the krona. It thus looks like a conflict between the establishment and the people, and certainly that was an important contributing element in the result. Among the adherents of all parties there was a substantial number resisting the euro. Resistance was overwhelmingly strong among the voters of the Centre Party (with 22 MPs), the Greens (17 MPs) and the Left (30 MPs), the parties that actually campaigned against the euro. But also a majority of the adherents of the governing Social Democrats (144 MPs) and the Christian Democrats (33 MPs) voted 'No', as did a quarter or more of the most committed pro-euro parties, the Conservatives (55 MPs) and the Liberals (48 MPs). However, the issue cannot simply be defined as a conflict between enlightened progress and the ignorant populace, as quite a few disillusioned commentators analyzed the result of the referendum. Even if 'Yes' received strong support by political parties and the Confederation of Swedish Enterprise, voices for 'No' were clearly heard also from within the establishment. For example, two former governors of *Riksbanken* (the Bank of Sweden), as well as individual representatives of business and academics, sided with 'No'.

Despite superior funding, 'Yes' failed to convince the majority. Officially reported figures indicate that 'Yes' had almost five times the financial resources of 'No' and, including funding that was not officially reported, the difference might have been as much as ten to one. There has been much dispute over what mistakes were made by the 'Yes' campaign, and these are blamed for the defeat. In fact, no mistakes can explain the failure; the causes lie in the unsound nature of the EMU project itself. There was a long campaign before the referendum. There is probably no other people, of any country in the EU, who know more about the construction of the EMU than the Swedes. The closest contenders would be the Danes who, in two referenda (1992 and 2000), have resisted the EMU.

The outcome of the Swedish referendum must be seen as an instance of rational expectations. The individual 'No' voices from within the establishment made clear that there was no obvious authority providing the right answer. And the arguments for the euro were simply not convincing.

It would be hard to demonstrate that the Swedish edition of this book, and the activities around it, had a measurable impact on the result. Yet, it might have contributed to some degree to show that doubts in the euro are not based on ignorance. Original versions of the chapters were presented at a workshop at Lund University in June 2003. The aim, then, was to add some critical aspects to the Swedish debate and to try to contribute to a political dialogue between citizens in a European context. Even now such dialogue is mostly reserved for those involved in the EU machinery, whether politicians or bureaucrats, and there is hardly any cross-border public debate.

Only minor revisions have been made in some of the chapters for the English edition. The book can thus provide evidence of the Swedish debate before the referendum. It might also contribute to the ongoing debate about the EMU in Britain and elsewhere. For example, the erosion of the Stability Pact in November 2003, when the Council overruled the Commission concerning the German and French violation of the budget rules, is more or less predicted and analyzed by several authors in this volume, before it happened.

This book is a joint venture supported by the efforts of all the contributors. But, of course, every author bears responsibility for his or her own chapter, which also should be obvious to the reader from the different views that are offered.

JONAS LJUNGBERG

1
Introduction

Jonas Ljungberg

Good ideas sometimes occur in the twilight. The origin of this book was in a discussion with James Foreman-Peck about the economic consequences of the introduction of the lira in 1861, due to the unification of Italy, previously so divided. Whether or not the lira can be blamed for the persistent gap between North and South in Italy, the common currency did not enhance the integration. Readers who are eager to take part of the argument about the Italian unification can turn to chapter seven, by Foreman-Peck.

In that discussion in February 2003 the idea arose for a European seminar and a book on the EMU. The point of departure was signalled in the working title, *The Case Against the EMU*.[1] As emphasized in the invitation to the seminar, it is not usual academic practice to define an established position in this way, but scholars also have responsibilities as citizens and the Swedish referendum about the euro was a reason for expressing these views in public. The seminar took place in Lund on 10 June, three months before the Swedish referendum on 14 September.

There were several reasons for assembling critical scholars. One was that the European integration has hardly given birth to a public political dialogue across national borders. We can take part of what is said on the political stage (well, at least a fraction), but the public discussion and comments are almost exclusively national. European affairs call for a European political dialogue among citizens. The seminar and the book were intended as a small contribution to such a dialogue.

Then why only critics? Big political projects with grand economic resources, like the European Union, also create huge service corps; that is, organizations and people whose behaviour and livelihood are, to a lesser or greater extent, dependent on the 'big project', and who naturally adjust themselves to its destination. Yet, there is also a need for a slave on the chariot, whispering to the emperor: 'Don't forget that you are mortal.'

Another reason for assembling critical scholars was the blunt interpretation of the opinion polls in the Swedish debate. Those who said 'Yes' to the euro were presented as well educated and with high income, whereas those who said 'No' were portrayed as less educated and low paid. As a corollary, more men would say 'Yes' and more women say 'No'. Our aim was to show that there are highly educated people, even specialists in the field, who consider the euro and its institutional framework perilous. Unfortunately, while emphasizing the message, the participants constituted a massive male majority which probably also contributes to our ignorance of an important feature of European integration: the handling of gender issues. Despite being a sign of political correctness in all other circumstances, this aspect almost became a blind spot in the debate. I will return to that issue below.

As regards criticism, it was not advice to the Swedish electorate that was asked for but different critical perspectives. The seminar stuck to the conventional academic process, undertaking critical evaluations of the arguments in the different papers, most of which appear in this book. As should be obvious to the reader, the contributors represent different theoretical opinions. One point of departure is in *public choice*, a theory that has nourished the arsenal of neoliberalism. Other criticism is built on the classical works of Keynes that provided the basis of the post-war welfare state. The opposite theories notwithstanding, conclusions about the EMU often are very similar and corroborate the criticism. The different perspectives are shown, for example, in the judgement on the European Central Bank (ECB) and the prospects for a change of its hard currency policy. The conclusion thereof, in particular concerning the risk of a financial crisis that grows with the inclusion also in the monetary union of the East European countries, must be taken seriously.

Now, what is all this about good ideas that occur in the twilight? It was not easy, at short notice, to gather scholars usually booked up semesters in advance. Nevertheless, the authors met on 10 June, joined by, among others, Nils Lundgren, Lars Pålsson-Syll and Lars Jonung, at the School of Economics in Lund – it was an open seminar. Some of the papers have been largely rewritten but in the main this book reproduces the presentations at the seminar. The short production time made it a limited project and several aspects of the euro are not dealt with.

The European perspective was new in the Swedish debate. Of course, Europe is habitually invoked, and our obligations towards Europe, but the direction or destination usually causes no concern. It is all about jumping on the bandwagon or whether there is any advantage from being on board. However, what is good for Europe is assumed mistakenly to be defined by Maastricht and other treaties. A European perspective also means a discussion among European citizens about the direction and destination of 'Europe'. That makes this book just as relevant after the Swedish referendum.

Euro: politics versus economics?

It is commonplace to divide the arguments about the EMU into political and economic. Some, for example Lars Calmfors, says that it is difficult to point out economic arguments for Sweden to adopt the euro but that the political arguments support such a step.[2] Similar voices were heard early in the debate: 'it should be for the Europeans themselves to decide whether there are net political advantages of EMU that outweigh the net economic disadvantages.'[3]

However, granted that the political arguments must be examined and ideologically evaluated, the distinction between politics and economics is illusory and many of the adherents of this view might be severely disappointed. That is the most important conclusion from the chapters in this book. Political solutions always have a price, more or less favourable, and economic solutions almost always affect politics. Thus the title of this book, *The Price of the Euro*. Some chapters, including this Introduction, are particularly focused on Sweden and the debate before the referendum on 14 September 2003. However, the chapter by Foreman-Peck is devoted to the British issue, and most chapters evaluate general aspects of the EMU. Thus the perspective is truly European.

The political argument: 'the idea of Europe'

One of the political arguments is that EMU should advance economic as well as political and, one might surmise, cultural integration in Europe. Despite that the start of the third step of the EMU, the introduction of the euro in January 2002, was conditional on economic *convergence*, equalization, among the participants, it does not follow that *divergence* has become impossible. On the contrary, the monetary union will probably sharpen the real economic differences between regions and countries in Europe. Changes in the exchange rate, now eliminated within the eurozone, have the function of smoothing variations in prices, earnings and living standards. This averaging effect not only operates in extreme cases with devaluations (or revaluations) which mark down (or mark up) a fixed exchange rate. The smoothing process also works with a floating exchange rate, normally with more gradual and marginal changes that can alleviate international differences in economic activity to some degree. That applies not the least when business cycles do not correspond between different currency areas. Several chapters deal to a greater or lesser extent with this problem. Chapter eight, written by this author, discusses how the long-term softening of the international value of the Swedish krona at the same time has sustained the domestic purchasing power of Swedish households.

If the new members of the European Union are allowed or required to adopt the euro relatively soon they must confront the problems arising from the permanently fixed exchange rate. The price level in these countries is today significantly lower than in Western Europe but they also have a higher inflation rate which, actually, means economic convergence, a levelling compared with the West. Within the EMU that implies a problem. First, at which exchange rate should they adopt the euro, and then, how should their inflation be handled?

As Roland Vaubel points out in chapter six, the East European inflation is structural and not easy to eliminate. This is why a higher inflation rate can be predicted into the future. Every solution has winners and losers, and this fact will certainly cause clashes that scarcely promote fraternity.

The first question is at which exchange rate the new members should adopt the euro. To start with a devaluation, that is adopting the euro at a low exchange rate, would stimulate the economic climate in the accession countries.[4] At the same time such a devaluation will increase the difference in price levels, measured in purchasing power parities, and hit competing firms in the West. Moreover, it will harm the self-confidence of the elite in these countries and maintain their image of being 'cousins from the countryside'. A huge devaluation (more than 15 per cent) would also violate the requirement for two years' 'exchange rate stability' before entrance, and can therefore be ruled out. A devaluation would, furthermore, increase the inflationary pressure which is contrary to the overriding aim of the EMU, and does not seem a probable solution. The Stability and Growth Pact (treated in depth in chapter three by Jespersen) would, in that case, backfire: the structural inflation pressure will be met by a deflationary economic policy.

Even if the euro is adopted at the existing exchange rate, are the new members likely to accede to demands for a deflationary policy that will depress economic growth? Poland is a case in point. Poland is, moreover, a weighty new member, with 39 million inhabitants (equal to Spain) – only Germany, Britain, France and Italy are more populous. Poland has 51 per cent of the population in the new member countries and 48 per cent of their GDP. The differences in economic structure compared with the West are striking: in 2000 GDP per capita was 39 per cent of that in the eurozone, and disposable income of the average household was less than half that in most old EU members. Unemployment exceeded 20 per cent in April 2003 against 8.8 per cent in the eurozone – average for the year 2000 was 16.4 per cent in Poland and 8.5 in the eurozone. The high unemployment in combination with a significantly lower male participation rate in the labour force, means that total employment is considerably lower in Poland than in the eurozone. The structural difference is emphasized by the fact that agriculture holds about 20 per cent of the labour force, and with a productivity only a fifth of that in other sectors of the Polish economy. Broadly speaking that means that the productivity of Polish agriculture is less than a sixth of that in Western Europe, and consequently convergence with the West will require a massive exodus from agriculture. A positive interpretation is that Poland has a big potential for catch-up with the West and for economic growth.

The situation presents a challenge that necessitates a tremendous transformation which for both economic and social reasons will take decades to achieve. This is where the Stability and Growth Pact enters the scene. With a budget deficit and a deficit in the current account, both taken as a share of GDP, as well as an inflation rate, above 5 per cent for several years, Poland and other new members will face demands for severe fiscal restraint.[5] This will impose a brake on economic growth, through deflationary pressure on the economy even if this does not necessarily show up in falling prices. And all this is futile, as highlighted by Swedish history in the half-century before World War I, with extremely fast economic growth, current account deficits and huge capital imports. Jesper Jespersen's description of the Stability and Growth Pact as a straitjacket is particularly pertinent for the new member countries. The combination of 'growth' and 'stability' is unfortunate, since sometimes economic growth requires that stability is broken. If stability is held as the overriding aim, it will sooner or later choke economic growth.

Renate Ohr, in chapter four, recognizes that the Eastern enlargement is a tough test for the monetary union and proposes that the inclusion of the new members in the EMU should wait until some other tests have been passed. If the new members are allowed to adopt the euro in the foreseeable future, the strains on the EMU will accumulate, as will the political contradictions within the EU. If they are not allowed to adopt the euro that will create an A team and a B team in the EU, 'a club in the club', to quote Renate Ohr. This is scarcely in line with the rhetoric of the idea of European unity. The assumption that the euro promotes political and cultural integration in Europe is thus a fragile foundation for the political argument.

The political argument: 'Solidarity'

A very popular version of the political argument, in Sweden, says that morally speaking we are obliged to adopt the euro. Some add that Sweden is legally obliged to do that. As members in the EU we should co-operate all the way and not live for ourselves. These are very compelling claims that must touch the heart of every upright citizen to some extent. Nevertheless they are, at least from a democratic point of view, false. The moral argument has nothing in common with liberal, nor with democratic, doctrine and rather is an echo of age-old state conservatism.

It is right that the EU has not given Sweden, like Britain and Denmark, any exemption from an introduction of the euro as soon as requirements are fulfilled. However, before the referendum on the EU membership, held on 13 November 1994, the protagonists replied to the warnings by the opponents to EMU that the membership in the monetary union was a question for the future that should not be confused with the contemporary referendum.[6] As such, that argument was deceitful and it was never endorsed by the European Commission, but as a consequence the alleged legal claim, that Sweden has to adopt the euro, has no democratic legitimacy.

The moral argument exists in several versions and they are all confusing. It is confusing to hear or read allegedly liberal-minded people stating that it is an 'obligation' to adopt the euro. Obligation to whom? To the idea of the state? Certainly not to the nation state, to which history has often given a democratic shape, but to a somewhat unknown European state. In the worst-case scenario that argument is a forerunner of totalitarian power. At least the moral argument has no restraints on such a development. Maybe it was that unwelcome insight that triggered the guardians of political correctness to call for self-criticism by Maud Olofsson (leader of the Centre Party) when she made a comparison between the EMU and the Third Reich during the political meetings in Almedalen.[7] She touched upon something indecent and very sensitive. It is not necessary to resort to such excessive arguments, even if associations easily emerge, when the dedication to Europe of the previous German chancellor Helmut Kohl is recalled: 'the implicit model may be Bismarck's ability to unify Germany around Prussia. As Chancellor Kohl frequently says, not without ambiguity, "Germany is our fatherland but Europe is our future." '[8]

Quite a few have warned about the 'democratic deficit' in the European Union.[9] Somehow the warnings are diminished through the assertion that the participating member countries are stable democracies and our expected loyalty is devoted towards them. Giscard d'Estaing's 'Convention for the Future of Europe' also has kept alive for a time the hope of democratic reform that should allow democratic control of the EU, similar to that of the democratic nation state. However, as long as bodies with only executive power in the nation states are granted legislative power in the union the 'deficit' will remain. Moreover, few have observed that the construction of the European Central Bank (ECB) actually has worsened the 'democratic deficit' in the EU. It must be noted that the ECB is a supranational authority that in itself is an element in the European state. A major cause of the emergence of the ECB is the movement in favour of central bank independence that swept over the Western world and, for example, increased the powers of the Bank of Sweden (*Riksbanken*) as formally enacted in 1999. However, James Forder remarks, in chapter five, that there is a fundamental difference between, on the one hand, the conditional independence of the Bank of Sweden and Bank of England and, on the other hand, the definite independence of the ECB. The latter should have *accountability* but Forder shows in detail that the ECB's interpretation and practice of that concept is far from the normal understanding of accountability under democratic control. One of Forder's points is that the policy of the ECB seems so much directed by its own interests as an organization, it develops a particular political culture and acts as an interest group within the European Union. Its political actions are not limited to the domain of monetary policy. In my own reading of Forder I cannot avoid recalling how the *Reichsbank*, under Hjalmar Schacht, contributed to the torpedoing of the feeble Weimar democracy, through political interventions that challenged the parliamentary government.[10]

Roland Vaubel, in his chapter, also discusses the ECB and the likelihood of a softening of its hard currency policy. Such a perspective does not change the problems of principles that Forder raises, although he, like many others, is critical of the hard currency policy. On the contrary, it confirms that there exists a political culture where decisions are determined by interest groups and groupings among countries rather than by an open discussion in an open society. When we couple the examinations by Forder and Vaubel with Lars E.O. Svensson's quiet but devastating criticism of the imprecise aim, and the both clumsy and closed construction of ECB,[11] then we have evidence of a serious threat against democracy.

What are these calls for 'solidarity' for our participation in that system? Could it be the solidarity with interest groups who look upon Brussels as the capital one must visit to join the gravy train? How many delegations from firms, government and organizations travel to the EU capital and which visions do they bear about an expanding business? It might be a necessary traffic yet we must also realize that here is an interest group that does not look upon its costs as a burden but as a growing plant, as the very aim. That interest group must be observed. In democracy politicians have to maximize their voters but here is a political field with seemingly unlimited prospects for growth and where, concomitantly, the role of the electorate is limited. Of course, the elite grind their teeth if they cannot participate wholly in the apportionment of that cake!

A more elevated version of the moral argument invokes Swedish neutrality during World War II. This version is even more confusing and one might ask for more considered thought. Of the present population of the eurozone, 47 per cent lives in Germany and Italy. How do the moralists perceive them? And the 15 per cent or so living in Austria, Greece, the former Vichy-France, states that more or less (as far as government resistance was concerned) were voluntarily occupied by the Nazis? Spain, Portugal and Ireland, like Sweden, said they were neutral. These parts of Europe account for more than 80 per cent of the population in the eurozone. Obviously the issue is not that easy. The Danish government co-operated with the occupiers, Norway resisted (Quisling, who headed a puppet government, was sentenced to death after the war) and Britain should pass the moral test almost without bad marks (the compromising Chamberlain was removed from power). Perhaps we had better ignore these countries since they have not joined the *single currency* (the rather Orwellian term now used to describe the common currency)! On the other hand, should not Denmark, Britain and Norway who are abiding with krona and pound also be ashamed?

Well, brief consideration demonstrates that it is not a constructive approach to history to relate the position towards EU and EMU to World War II and the neutrality of a country like Sweden. Is it a recovery of the activist policy during the Thirty Years' War that some Swedes are recollecting? Or, is it a desire for a European super-power in the making?

Politics, economy, culture: the manifold nature of Europe

The American Challenge was the title of a bestseller by the French publicist Jean-Jacques Servan-Schreiber in the late 1960s.[12] The book appeared precisely at the right point in time. After two decades of more rapid economic growth in Europe, American superiority had been eroded to a large degree. The US was under vigorous pressure due to the Vietnam War. In a few years a currency crisis would force a devaluation of the dollar and a breakdown of the fixed exchange rates of the Bretton Woods system.[13] Yet, despite the crisis of the 1970s damaging high growth rates, full employment in Europe and bitter defeat in Vietnam, the US continued to proceed along its historical trend as regards economic growth. Servan-Schreiber called for a new European strategy, or, more correctly, *one* strategy instead of European division in order to economically and politically compete with the US. In chapter nine, Hans Albin Larsson raises these issues from a political perspective. A European rivalry with the US is not a serious alternative but a Utopia for the federalists, according to Larsson. Maybe one reason is, as pointed out in chapter two, by Arjo Klamer, that the American citizen pays three times as much as the French or German citizen for their armed forces.

Even if the European super state might be a Utopia, the monetary union is seen by Larsson as a step towards centralization and levelling of distinctions. The driving force behind this development he finds in the inherited great power ambitions of France. The Gaullism, often conceived as narrowly nationalist, is here unexpectedly but reasonably comprehended as the strategist of the idea of Europe.

Larsson's interpretation of the history and future of the European Union is, from another angle, supported by chapter seven. However, it is scarcely controversial to assert that the old project with a monetary union could be realized first through, what I dare denominate *imperial* agreement between Chancellor Kohl and President Mitterrand. By relinquishing *Bundesbank* hegemony among the central banks Kohl could get the compliance of Mitterrand for the German reunification. Despite the fact that Germany now has a population a third larger than any of the three other big member countries, her voting power has not become heavier within the EU. On the other hand, the loss was not that heavy: from the *Bundesbank*, at Wilhelm-Epstein Strasse, there are not many steps to Kaiserstrasse and ECB – in Frankfurt, of course.

The driving force of France in the EU and EMU is certainly a strong and extraordinarily important factor, yet how come so many can be so attracted by the idea of Europe? The American challenge is probably another factor, whether as a Utopia or as an counterweight. The idea of 'the United States of Europe' surfaced a couple of times during the 20th century, only to disappear again. Winston Churchill held up that idea for a while after World War II, before the orientation towards the Commonwealth regained its supremacy, for reasons that

Foreman-Peck highlights. However, the development going on in the EU and EMU requires more than a general opinion, especially since that opinion in many member countries often must be won by hook and by crook. There must be a strong *actor* for more supranational government and a stronger central power, an actor for a European government. Such an aim scarcely has any attraction among the broad spectrum of citizens. But for those more or less involved in the processes, or hoping for a chance to get there, this is an irresistible cause. It concerns an interest group with its centre in Brussels and branches in all countries. The enlargement of the circle of members then can be perceived as a way both to maximize the support for the interest group and to make its accountability more unapproachable.

Against the centralist trend Larsson makes a call for a decentralized, pluralist alternative for the European Union. A few of the authors, and in particular Foreman-Peck, outline a strategy aimed at that alternative. It is about institutional competition. British, as well as Swedish, solutions of economic policy should be used and allowed to exist side by side with the continental models. Progress diffuses when successful solutions are borrowed across borders. Real influence can be gained in this way, points out Foreman-Peck, whereas membership in the eurozone only brings the illusory influence of one in the row.

Are Larsson and Foreman-Peck realists, is institutional competition a possibility? Arjo Klamer, in chapter two, twists the question: is the centralization in a borderless European state sustainable? Differences of language and culture are realities that do not seem to be levelled down in the course of time. Despite globalization the number of nation states is increasing. Decolonization and the fall of the Soviet and Tito powers offer important examples confirming the difficulty of eradicating national differences. Regionalization is the reply of EU, and is supposed to bridge the gap between local community and central authority when the nation state is fading away. With monetary union, however, the centrifugal forces in the system increase and Klamer predicts its failure. Preceding monetary unions have been sustainable only when constructed within some sort of nation state, such as the US and Germany, whereas others have dissolved. The road to dissolution also seems unattractive. It will be adjoined by controversies between centralism and national and populist interests.

Would decentralism and institutional competition be an answer to the American challenge? As emphasized by Foreman-Peck, exactly such factors can explain the historical divide between Europe and, for example, China. It is well known that many technical inventions were first launched in China but the monolithic empire stifled sustainable development and economic growth. The institutional diversity in Europe, on the contrary, promoted transformation and progress. Foreman-Peck's argument is that even today reforms are more smoothly accomplished within the nation state, while the institutional yardstick within the EU, for example, as regards the labour market, is set by the least flexible country. That idea is not uncontroversial but if it is correct it damages one of the main arguments in favour of the euro, as held by the Confederation of Swedish Enterprise. Moreover, it would also imply that Italy or Ireland set the standard as regards the social position of women – an issue further discussed below.

Centralization around a European government means, from this perspective, stagnation and not an adequate response to the American challenge. That is also the usual fate for grand political projects: the proud aim in fact achieves the opposite. Just this historical experience should make us careful with the euro even if it is wrapped in enticing words like 'the idea of Europe' or 'a peace project'.

Are the costs of the Euro measurable?

It is commonplace, even among experts, to suggest that the economic consequences of the Euro are unpredictable.[14] If by this is meant that the future is unpredictable, then the suggestion is, of course, true. For example, at the end of World War II few believed in a long period of high economic growth. Economists predicted a depression.[15] That concern was fortunate because much activity was directed towards the prevention of a new depression. The post-war international economic regime, with Bretton Woods, GATT and the Marshall Plan, grew from such efforts and maybe thereby a depression was avoided.

That case highlights that the future is difficult to predict, yet it is possible to know the role of different factors and activities. It is possible to know direction of the impact of the euro; however, since all acting and counteracting forces are not known, we are not able exactly to predict the outcome. It is possible to show that the euro would be a brake on economic growth in Poland but if the growth forces are strong enough, Poland will, nevertheless, improve its economic position. However, in that case it will be *despite* the euro.

It is possible to make an account of the benefits and costs of the euro for Sweden but, this notwithstanding, it will be difficult in the future to measure the outcome. It will still be a matter of conjecture what would have happened if another road had been taken, although it is possible to compare countries in the eurozone with those outside. The latter comparison is performed in the chapters by Jespersen, Foreman-Peck and this author. The more conjectural sort of comparison follows in the sections below, with an assessment of the benefits and costs of the euro for Sweden. Simplifying somewhat, it is assumed that benefits are resources that could be directed to consumption and investments and correspondingly increase GDP, whereas costs are drawn from consumption and investments and thus reduce GDP. The calculations pertain to Swedish GDP in 2002 that amounted to 2,430 million kronor and, when not otherwise stated, other figures mentioned also pertain to 2002.

Euro benefit: lower transaction costs

Until recently transaction costs due to currency exchange and currency insurance were judged rather insignificant. Those costs include financial operations such as futures and hedging to fence off exchange rate variations between the point in time of contract and delivery or payment. The public report on Sweden and the EMU in 1996 estimated these transaction costs of Sweden's trade with other EU to 0.2 per cent of GDP,[16] corresponding to 4.9 billion kronor in 2002. Since some of these financial services are performed in Sweden it is a simplification to count this money as a possible increase of GDP. Yet, costs of business should be lowered; let us treat that as a common interest. Another point is that the trade with Britain and Denmark is included and since exchange transactions with these countries would remain the benefits should be reduced. The British and Danish shares in Swedish foreign trade are 20 per cent compared with 74 per cent for all EU. Benefits should be reduced by at least a quarter to 3.6 billion kronor or 0.15 per cent of GDP.

It is often suggested that the euro will increase competition in the Swedish domestic market and bring about lower prices in retail trade. The reason should be lower transaction costs but it is somewhat obscure why prices should be lower when counted in euros instead of kronor. In order to make the argument convincing one has to explain why food prices are about 10 per cent lower in Gothenburg than in Stockholm.

Anecdotal evidence can be telling, as this story is about gasoline prices. The weekend before midsummer I passed through Bromölla, a southern village, on the highway. The gas station on the south side of the highway had a big sign announcing the price, 8.79, but surprisingly the gas station on the north side of the highway announced 9.29. A price difference of 0.50 kronor per litre of exactly the same commodity and with the same availability (there is no fence on the highway) should quickly be levelled out. Two weeks later I passed Bromölla on the highway once again and the expensive gasoline on the north side actually had decreased by 0.05 to 9.24 kronor. However, the cheap gasoline on the south side had decreased six times as much, and now cost 8.49, widening the price gap to 0.75 kronor. It is hard to believe that counting in euros would make a difference in cases like this. In other words, there are more factors than the currency that determine competitive or non-competitive behaviour.

Euro benefit: increasing trade

As highlighted in the Swedish debate, recent research has come up with evidence indicating substantial gains from a common currency.[17] According to a recent study of the 1970s and 1980s, trade between countries that adopted a common currency increased radically more than between countries that did not adopt a common currency.[18] However, contained in that result are several problems that can be summarized in a sentence every scholar must never forget: correlation or a statistical relation between two phenomena does not make up a causality. Moreover, specialists do not even agree that the correlation in the case of the role of currency unions in world trade in the 1970s and 1980s is statistically significant.[19] Concerning causality, there are other factors that influence the outcome – the common currency can, as should be well known, be part of a broader co-operation. Most of the evidence is brought up by small countries in the Third World where quite ordinary changes add up to a big per centage change. That, as well as the shakiness of the result, is illustrated by the fact that the impact of the common currency varies from a 13–700 per cent increase of foreign trade![20] Another flaw in the argument of the beneficial trade hypothesis is that a common currency should also increase trade with countries outside the currency area. In experimental science a control sample without the examined characteristic, here the common currency, should warn about spurious correlation and indicate that there are other explanatory variables, apart from those included in the model, which influence the result. The adherents of the beneficial trade hypothesis believe, however, that the spurious correlation corroborates the hypothesis.

As an exercise, though, assume that the recent results about the beneficial effects on international trade of the common currency are about correct. Assume that Swedish trade with the eurozone increases 20 per cent.[21] That would be equivalent to an increase in exports of 62 billion kronor, based on figures for 2001.[22] However, the increase in exports are gross values and these do not equal the amount that would be added to GDP. GDP is composed of value added, in this case the sales or gross values less intermediate goods. Value added on average makes up about 35 per cent of manufacturing sales and if we assume that the share is somewhat higher in exports, a reasonable maximum figure of value added for the new exports is 25 billion kronor. The increase in exports would thus add 25 billion or roughly 1 per cent to GDP.[23]

Since the common currency would symmetrically enhance trade between the involved countries, an equiproportionate increase in imports must be assumed. Swedish imports from the eurozone are higher than exports and 20 per cent should add up to 64 billion kronor. Since the increase of exports was 62 billion, the common currency would, thus assumed, slightly impair the Swedish current account. Just as more Swedish exports to the eurozone will partly replace domestic production elsewhere, correspondingly increasing imports will out-compete domestic production here. To the extent that the imports mean higher consumption and investment, that is, not only substitute domestic production, it has to be paid for out of an increment to GDP, if it is not just to be a levy on the current account. Therefore, it is reasonable to assume that this part of the new imports corresponds to the value added of the new exports, assumed to be 25 billion kronor. The remaining 39 billion kronor new imports would then substitute domestic production. Say that value added of these domestically produced goods is a third of sales values, or 13 billion kronor. The substitution effect of increased imports would thus imply a deduction from GDP of 13 billion kronor. The combined impact on

GDP of the 20 per cent increase in exports and imports would then be a plus of 25 billion and a minus of 13 billion, adding up to an increase of 12 billion kronor or 0.5 per cent of GDP.

Consumers will find more advantages from an increase in trade since commodities will become cheaper and that will also have a positive impact on resource allocation and consequently on economic growth. This impact on growth is, however, very marginal since what has been discussed above is a threshold effect on trade with the adoption of the euro and not an effect that grows year by year. There are also social costs connected with the substitution of imports for domestic production, costs that become higher the more sudden the replacement.

There are other important aspects of Swedish foreign trade. As regards exports and economic growth it matters in which markets Swedish industry has been expanding over time. Probably the products sold at those markets have represented the best productivity performance in Swedish industry. It has been shown that, in the very long term at least, a higher growth in output for a product or a branch of industry goes hand in hand with a more rapid increase in its productivity.[24] Then, a look at the distribution of Swedish exports shows a decreasing trend of the share going to countries presently in the European Union. In 1980 their share in Swedish exports was 77 per cent; in 1994, the year before Sweden entered EU, it was 75 per cent; and in 2001 it had further decreased to 70 per cent. The present eurozone took 53 per cent in 1980 and 1994, and 51 per cent in 2001. The share of exports directed to the world outside EU and neighbouring Norway has increased from 10 per cent in 1980, to 15 per cent in 1994 and 19 per cent in 2001.

Most of the exports to the 'outside world' go to countries that more or less belong to the dollar area. Consequently Swedish progressive export interests probably are better served by a currency that floats between the euro and the dollar, than by a fixed exchange rate to either. Foreman-Peck argues that this is also the case for Britain – for Sweden the pound could be added to the euro and the dollar.

In conclusion, the benefits for the Swedish economy of the impact of the euro on foreign trade are very uncertain. If we accept the beneficial trade hypothesis, and assume a 20 per cent increase of the trade with the eurozone, it will reasonably add 12 billion kronor or 0.5 per cent to Swedish GDP, when account is taken of intermediate goods and the increase not only of exports but also of imports. It must be reiterated, however, that the 'last word' in research, as in fashion, is not always sustainable and the beneficial trade hypothesis does not seem to have good chances for survival. Its surfacing in the Swedish debate obviously has much to do with the support from a powerful interest group, the Confederation of Swedish Enterprise.

Euro benefit: less currency speculation

Perhaps the most compelling economic argument in favour of a common currency is that it would eliminate currency speculation. Then, what is currency speculation? It is large and fast capital movements that worsen a financial crisis and torpedo the exchange rate. In the post-war period, national restrictions on international capital flows limited the occurrence and diffusion of financial crises. That changed when, in particular during the 1980s, many countries opened their national capital markets and international financial markets grew explosively. In the autumn of 1992, along with several European countries, Sweden suffered from the so-called EMS crisis with devastating effects.[25] That experience has nourished the hope that the euro will provide security.

Basically, the reason for flight from a currency is loss of confidence. Among the common causes a few could be emphasized: 1) worsening deficit in the current account caused by an overvaluation of the currency of the country; 2) large short-term loans that are not sufficiently backed by the reserve of foreign currencies; 3) lacking information, inadequate supervision of the financial sector or corruption has led to an accumulation of bad loans; 4) a rapid increase of an already large government debt.

Usually different causes underpin each other, yet often with an overvalued currency (point 1) as the key factor. The overvaluation is dependent on an arrangement where the currency is linked to other currencies in a fixed exchange rate. For example, the Swedish krona was very unsuccessfully locked within the European Exchange Rate Mechanism (ERM) in May 1991, at a point in time when the deflationary crisis gained momentum on the heavily indebted real estate market. When the fixed exchange rate within the ERM was left in November 1992 the krona, in a few months, fell 33 per cent against the US dollar and 25 per cent against the Deutschmark.

In the Asian crisis points 2 and 3 played a crucial role, but also here a fixed exchange rate was a key factor that in several countries gave wealthy actors an escape hatch before the devaluation was finally undertaken. The latest big currency crisis emerged in Argentina in 2001. Once again it was a fixed exchange rate, the locking of the peso to the US dollar, that piece by piece impaired competitiveness and brought a disastrous failure. Point 4 is exemplified by the French crisis in 1981, when an expansionary budgetary policy undermined the trust of the financial markets in the French franc. However, in this case there was also a fixed alignment within the European Monetary System that made the target much more clear-cut.

A conclusion is that a floating exchange rate, which Sweden has had since 1992, is the best though not a guaranteed insurance against currency crisis, or destabilizing speculation. In addition, a sound economy is also necessary. However, with a fixed exchange rate the constraints are much more severe. That is also the motivation for the present hard currency policy of the ECB but both Vaubel and Ohr see a danger that a weakening of this position will expose even the euro to vicious capital movements. Trust in the euro and the ECB will then erode, the more so if new members adopt the euro and the disparities within the eurozone grow. This will increase pressure on the whole eurozone, with demands for higher interest rates from financial markets, and that will be a threat for the sustainability of the euro.

Thus, the alleged benefit of reduced currency speculation is questionable. Actually, the choice is about weighing risks connected with unknown and different events. Yet, a reasonable judgement is that the prospects for managing speculation are greater with the krona, especially if it is allowed to float, and the downside risks consequently reduced.

Euro cost: changeover costs

Despite meticulous examination of various aspects, the public EMU reports almost ignored the changeover costs. These pertain to cash registers and IT systems, book-keeping, mark-ups, planning and training of personnel etc.[26] Thus there exists no total estimate or calculation of changeover costs for all the sectors of the economy, such as trade and private services, manufacturing and the government.

Nevertheless, the costs are not trivial, as indicated by a range of sources. The daily press reported investigations concerning the retail trade and some public institutions. For example, the institution handling student allowances (*Centrala studiestödsnämnden, CSN*) estimated that they would need 200 extra personnel for one year to manage the changeover to the euro. Other public institutions were said to agree that the changes would be much greater than with the once anticipated IT horrors of the new millennium. Most remarkable, however, was that the Cabinet shrugged their shoulders. Changeover costs must be financed within the ordinary budget limits, they said. The nonchalance might be based on the conception of a once-and-for-all cost. That was the thrust of the public EMU report repeated by Professor Calmfors in a comment on the estimates by the public institutions.[27] Other authors found consolation in that concept: 'fortunately it is a once-and-for-all cost by contrast to the current costs of currency exchanges.'[28]

Economic theory, however, recognizes that 'once-and-for-all costs' have an equivalent annual cost. In both cases the relevant economic concept is opportunity cost. For example, the opportunity cost of 200 extra positions at CSN equals allowances for roughly 1,000 students for one year. In other words, that equals financial support that would enable more than 300 students to take their Bachelor degree. The example illustrates that the changeover costs not only have an opportunity cost but also a dynamic impact that does not vanish in the foreseeable future. The more than 300 graduates would give a greater contribution to the economy than without their three years at university and a degree.

Although the euro is now in its second year as a circulating currency, valid calculations of the actual changeover costs are scarce. In the Netherlands, however, changeover costs have been estimated at 1.1 per cent of GDP.[29] Foreman-Peck cites an estimate endorsed by a British parliamentary committee as high as £30 billion, broadly speaking 3 per cent of the British GDP. That might sound excessive but the figure is not plucked from the air; the experience of the changeover from the archaic pounds, shillings and pence system (LSD) to the decimal system in 1971 can be drawn on.

If Swedish changeover costs arrive somewhere between the actual Dutch and the predicted British numbers, that is between 1.1 and 3 per cent of GDP, then the bill will not be less than 27 billion kronor and might approach 73 billion. At least a third will pertain to the public sector and must be financed through taxes. Even if we call it a once-and-for-all tax, the amount 9–24 billion kronor is hardly trivial. Who should pay? Evenly distributed, every one of the almost 4 million Swedish households would be billed for between 2,300 and 6,000 kronor, roughly the cost of one month's food consumption in a family. And this will only cover adopting the euro in the public sector.

The other 18–48 billion kronor are higher business costs and higher prices for consumers. Equally distributed this is equivalent to 4,600–12,000 kronor per household. There would be barely any doubt about the outcome of the referendum if the question was put: 'Are you and your family prepared to pay a 'once-and-for-all cost' of 6,900–18,000 kronor in order to be entitled to use the euro as a means of payment?' The annual interest of that sum, if placed in a sound bank, would be enough to pay for the exchange costs on the holiday trip, and probably more than that.

Another aspect is the dynamic effect of the changeover costs, as discussed for the British case by Foreman-Peck. The dynamic effect is the changeover costs recalculated as annual payments, just as is usually done with investments. One should note, though, that the same reservation applies as in the case of transaction costs. Changeover costs will be paid for services that contribute to GDP and therefore the aggregate economy does not suffer an equally big loss, even if it is a serious misallocation. The opportunity cost is thus relevant and, when asked, most people would probably prefer not to spend in this way on changeover. The value thereof can be shown by a cost-benefit estimate. At a discount rate of 3.5 per cent the 'once-and-for-all' cost of 27 billion would equal a perpetual, annual expenditure of 950 million kronor, and with a 'once-and-for-all' cost of 73 billion the annual fee would be 2.6 billion.

Euro cost: higher taxes

The preceding section showed that already the change from krona to euro would require a not insignificant tax increase, unless the non-chalance of the Department of Finance hides a plan to cut other government expenditures. Anyway, it becomes ever more obvious that the euro will bring about tax increases. Already the first public EMU report has advocated a strengthening of government finances. Now Assar Lindbeck advocates the same, 'as an action of preparedness'.[30] What can be expected with the euro was finally made clear by the joint manoeuvre in the campaign by Prime Minister Persson and Trade Union President Wanja Lundby-Wedin.[31] The governing Social Democratic Party then suggested that the target of a budgetary surplus should be increased from 2 per cent to 2.5 per cent of GDP, and the surplus should be used for amortization of the public debt. This increase of 0.5 per cent amounts to 12 billion kronor or, equally distributed, 3,300 kronor per household. It might seem sound to pay off the public debt since it reduces government interest costs, and boosts confidence in Sweden's creditworthiness, which will lower the interest rate, cure the economic activity or enhance further borrowing. However, that is disregarding other circumstances, such as welfare needs and the single interest rate of the eurozone, which mean that an amortization may not necessarily be appropriate in a given situation.

This extra amortization should be an insurance against the hazards of the euro and a substitute for the loss of the monetary and currency policy. Thus, it is a price label for the stability costs of the euro, suggested by advocates of the euro. The direct impact is an increase of taxes, unless the money is provided by reductions of other public expenditure. The effect on interest costs and the interest rate is, however, modified by an immediate reduction of consumption and investments, the greater the amortization that is paid on foreign debt. In any case, the increase of taxes will reduce households' consumption and increase the liquidity of the financial enterprises that hold the majority of government bonds, and most likely the effect will be a reduction of the aggregate economic activity. Given the high tax pressure in Sweden it is remarkable that so many parties and interest groups seem to acquiesce in a further increase, only to accommodate the euro.

Despite those clear signals there exists a general expectation that EMU in the somewhat longer term will enforce 'harmonization' of budgetary and tax policy, and thereby alleviate the tax pressure in Sweden. However, if resources are not increased through high economic growth, a reduction of the tax pressure will necessitate drastic cuts in public services or in public transfers like pensions, and allowances for unemployed, students, new parents etc.

If such changes are desirable, why should they be enforced through 'harmonization' within the EMU and not through democratic decisions, in the parliament through 'the age-old right of the Swedish people to tax itself', as stated in the old constitution? National differences in the size of the public sector, and in the tax pressure, have deeper historical and social roots than programmes of political parties. In the case of Sweden, for example the Poor Law of 1918 can be seen as path-breaking in enacting the responsibility of the local governments to take care of elderly people. Until the 1950s the Swedish public sector, as a share of GDP, was modest in international comparison. But when Sweden, in the 1960s (before other countries), attained a high proportion of people over the age of 65, the solution was provided by previous historical crossroads and traditions. The welfare state and not the family became the response to, *inter alia*, the expansion of ageing. Since the major part of the labour force in public services are women, the female participation ratio in the labour market also increased rapidly.[32] From a level distinctly below the average among industrialized countries in 1950, the share of females in the Swedish labour market rose to the highest in the world in the 1970s. A slight reduction has recently taken place, yet the latest data from OECD indicate that 76 per cent of Swedish women are working outside the household, compared to an average of 58 per cent in the eurozone, with 48 per cent in Italy the lowest figure.[33] It is plainly evident that these differences reflect diverse ways of living and it must be questioned whether a single European lifestyle could be so smoothly imposed as pretended by the words 'tax harmonization'. For example, do Swedish women want to abstain from the independence provided by a job?

As mentioned in the chapter by Forder, there are already suggestions from the ECB about public service cuts. Should Prime Minister Göran Persson try to realize his prediction of 108,000 new public jobs with the Swedish adoption of the euro,[34] he will face fierce opposition from several fellow Europeans who will not find that this fits with 'harmonization'.

Conclusions concerning the economic consequences of the tax effects of the euro are, first, that the raising of the budgetary surplus will be a brake on economic growth. Second, the long-term consequences of an anticipated tax harmonization within the eurozone will have pervasive economic and social impacts that are not easily calculated. The structural changes may be large without actually enhancing economic growth. A 'harmonization' that induces a lower (female) employment will reduce economic growth.

A 'harmonization' of family policy would also have important repercussions. In 1990 Sweden had the highest fertility ratio in Europe (except Iceland), 2.13 children per woman. In 1990, only Sweden had not faced falling fertility since the 1960s. With cuts in social benefits during the 1990s, such as the parental allowances, the fertility ratio fell to 1.54, broadly in line with the EU average of 1.53. Still there is some way to go before reaching the levels of Spain and Italy, with fertility ratios of 1.22 and 1.25, respectively. Considering that people are living ever longer and that the proportion of elderly people is ever increasing, falling fertility ratios are a serious problem for long-term economic growth.

Euro cost: income of the Riksbanken

To run a central bank is a profitable business, partly due to the *seignorage* that is generated through the emission of notes and sometimes also coins. The monies are not, of course, distributed for nothing; for example, *Riksbanken* (Bank of Sweden) buys financial assets whereby notes are used as payment and thus circulated. In the eurozone the ECB takes care of this business but the revenue is redistributed according to the member countries' shares in the ECB, which have been determined by population and GDP. As a member of the EMU, although not having implemented its third stage or the adoption of the euro, Sweden, or the *Riksbanken*, has a share of 2.65 per cent in the ECB. For 2002 the ECB redistributed 614 million euro to the national central banks, as a result of the issue of euro notes.[35] Assume that the sum would have been 2.65 per cent higher, totalling 630 million euro, had Sweden also adopted the euro. Then the *Riksbanken*'s share in the redistributed profit would have amounted to 16.7 million euro or about 150 million kronor.

Evidence shows that forgone revenues of the *Riksbanken* would result in a substantial cost for Swedish tax payers. As a rule the *Riksbanken* annually delivers 80 per cent of its last five years' average profit, exclusive of exchange rate effects, to the government. Over the period 1993–2002, the *Riksbanken* thus handed over 74.9 billion kronor to the Minister of Finance. Even in 1994, when the *Riksbanken* lost more than 12 billion, 6.2 billion were delivered, and in 2002, with a loss of 71 million, 7.3 billion were paid over. The average delivered during 1998–2002 amounted to 8.4 billion kronor annually; it seems reasonable to conclude that with the adoption of the euro not even a fraction of this amount would be passed over to the Swedish government.

In this exercise, the fact that the total profits of the *Riksbanken* were higher than those revenues delivered to the government has been disregarded. Thus, whereas this latter sum amounted to 74.9 billion for the period 1993–2002, the profits totalled 128 billion kronor.[36] It is thus a fairly modest estimate to conclude that it would cost the Swedish economy 8 billion kronor annually, or 0.33 per cent of GDP, to degrade the national central bank to a local branch of the ECB.

The price of the euro – and of the krona

Table 1.1 summarizes the benefits of the euro as the price that must be paid for keeping the krona, and the costs of adopting the euro equal the price of the 'single currency'. The reservations, made at the outset of the whole exercise, must be kept in mind. Some costs are not equal to a loss in GDP but would, in part, be a redistribution within society. That applies both to exchange transactions and tax increases, and also to changeover costs. Note also that changeover costs are recalculated as annual payments on the lower estimate, 27 billion kronor, of the bill for adopting the euro. The redistributive impact of the changeover cost is underrated since it will be laid on firms, consumers and taxpayers at once. On the other hand, the

Table 1.1 The cost of the euro compared with the krona

Annual cost	Krona		Euro	
	Billion SEK	per cent of GDP	Billion SEK	per cent of GDP
Exchange transactions	3.6	0.15		
'Currency speculation'	?	?	?!	?!
Forgone Increase of trade	12	0.50		
Changeover			1.0	0.04
Tax increase			12	0.50
Revenue of the *Riksbanken*			8	0.33
Total	15.6	0.65	21	0.87

impact of the euro through foreign trade is probably overrated and also hides redistributive effects. Table 1.1 thus can scarcely be said to idealize the benefits of the krona.

The bottom line shows that the price of the euro is higher than of retaining the krona. However, the calculation is simplistic since some effects are difficult to quantify. For example, 'currency speculation' has been denoted with question marks because such events are hard to predict due to, for example, policy decisions. However, as argued above, the euro seems more hazardous and the exclamation marks indicate that the EMU is, quoting the Prime Minister, 'a shaky project'.[37]

There are also other economic aspects not considered in Table 1.1. For example, chapters in this book discuss problems such as the deflationary pressure that the euro would impose on Sweden (Vaubel), the difficulties of performing economic policy (Jespersen, Forder, Foreman-Peck) and the risks of a crisis of the EMU (Klamer, Ohr). Another problem that largely has been ignored in the Swedish debate concerns the exchange rate at which the euro should be adopted. Since the krona is floating, the exchange rate has to be locked to the euro for two years before the changeover to the common currency. In the case of a 'Yes' in the referendum, one could expect an immediate locking of the krona to the euro. At which rate?

In December 2002, the average figure predicted by the four large Swedish banks was 8.65 kronor per euro.[38] In that month the actual exchange rate was, on average, 9.09 which implies a revaluation of 5 per cent. A revaluation means that Swedish enterprises have to reduce their prices if they are to keep their competitiveness in both export markets and the import-competing part of the domestic market. That is equal to a pressure on wages and other costs as well as on profitability. The exchange rate will be decided through negotiations; some actors want an even tougher revaluation. For example the Union of Metalworkers in Finland, in an intervention on Reuters' web debate, claimed that the krona should be locked at 8.00 to 8.40 to the euro.[39] The exchange rate issue is another reason why one should doubt the beneficial trade hypothesis. With a revalued exchange rate exports will get into difficulties, whereas imports will increase. It seems probable, therefore, that the euro will favour imports but not exports – scarcely a recipe for economic growth.

Finally, just as the risk of 'currency speculation' is difficult to quantify so are the political issues. Yet, chapters in this book emphasize that the political price of the euro is costly, far too costly.

Notes

1. Almost the same title, 'The Case Against EMU', was used before, by Martin Feldstein, *The Economist*, 13 June 1992, pp. 12–19. In general American economists seem to have been more outspoken about EMU than European colleagues. For example, at Lund University in 1997 a paper was presented by Larry Neal, with the (today) politically incorrect title 'An American's Perspective on the European Monetary Union: Deutschemark über alles'. See also L. Neal and D. Barbezat, *The Economics of the European Union and the Economies of Europe*, New York: Oxford Univesity Press, 1998. However, it has been considered important here only to include the views of Europeans as those concerned.
2. 'EMU does not boost the economy', *Svenska Dagbladet*, 22 November 2002; 'Erroneous promises about higher employment', *Dagens Nyheter*, 4 July 2003. Professor Calmfors is particularly associated with the impressive public EMU reports, *SOU 1996*: 158; *SOU 2000*: 16.
3. M. Feldstein, 'The Political Economy of the European Economic and Monetary Union: Political Sources of an Economic Liability', *Journal of Economic Perspectives*, 11 (4), 1997, p. 24.
4. Compare with the devaluation of about 30 per cent of the West European currencies against the US dollar in 1949, during the introduction of the Bretton Woods monetary regime – briefly discussed in chapter eight.
5. Data on Poland and other countries from OECD, *Main Economic Indicators*, 'Basic structural statistics', December 2002, and 'Standardised unemployment rates', June 2003; M. Ådahl and J. Eklund, *Allt om EMU*, Stockholm: SNS 2003; D. Turnock, *The East European Economy in Context. Communism and Transition*, London: Routledge, 1997.
6. One example, among various: 'Sweden can remain outside EMU', editorial in *Sydsvenska Dagbladet*, 9 November 1994. The leaflet, sent by the Foreign Ministry to all households, stated: 'The parliament will decide on the participation in a common currency.' Later on the leader of the conservative party, Carl Bildt, launched the idea of a referendum about the euro.
7. Almedalen, in Gotland, has, since the days of Olof Palme, been a regular scene, each summer, for political speeches and meetings; these hit an 'all time high' before the referendum in 2003. Maud Olofsson's utterance was actually an uncritical comment to an intervention by Janet Bush from the British 'No' campaign.
8. Feldstein, 'The Political Economy of the European Economic and Monetary Union: Political Sources of an Economic Liability', p. 29.
9. The origin of the 'democratic deficit' is explained in chapter nine, by Hans Albin Larsson.

10. H. Müller, *Die Zentralbank – eine Nebenregierung: Reichsbankspräsident Hjalmar Schacht als Politiker der Weimarer Republik*, Opladen: Westdeutscher Verlag, 1973.
11. L.E.O. Svensson, 'Sverige, valutaunionen och penningpolitiken', *Ekonomisk Debatt*, 4, 2003, pp. 50–2.
12. J.J. Servan-Schreiber, *Le défi américain*, Paris: Denoël, 1967 (English edition, 1968).
13. Regarding monetary regimes, see chapter eight.
14. The prime public EMU investigator, professor Calmfors, has been mentioned; another is C. Wyplozs, 'EMU: Why and How It Might Happen', *Journal of Economic Perspectives*, 11 (4), 1997, pp. 3–22.
15. See, for example, G. Myrdal, *Varning för fredsoptimism!*, Stockholm: Albert Bonniers förlag, 1944.
16. *SOU 1996: 158*, p. 403.
17. See, for example, P. Braunerhjelm (ed.), *Därför euron. Tio ekonomer om den gemensamma valutan*, Stockholm: Ekerlids, 2003.
18. A. Rose, 'One money, one market: the effect of common currencies on trade', *Economic Policy*, 30, 2000, pp. 9–45.
19. T. Persson, 'Currency unions and trade: how large is the treatment effect?', *Economic Policy*, 31, 2001, pp. 435–48.
20. H. Flam, 'Handel och medlemskap i EMU', *Ekonomisk debatt*, 4, 2003, p. 71.
21. Although Rose, in a pamphlet, 'EMU and Swedish Trade', published by the Confederation of Swedish Enterprise (2001), seems to predict an increase of 50 per cent.
22. Data on Swedish foreign trade here and below from *SOS, Utrikeshandel*, annually up to 2001.
23. Value added for exports is not reported in the National Accounts, and the assumed 40 per cent value added in gross values is higher than the average for manufacturing.
24. J. Ljungberg, *Priser och marknadskrafter i Sverige 1885–1969. En prishistorisk studie*, Lund: Ekonomisk-historiska Föreningen, 1990.
25. The EMS crisis is covered in more detail in chapter eight.
26. 'The once-and-for-all costs connected with the transition should be deducted [from the benefits]. These are difficult to estimate. According to one estimate, the total costs of changing IT systems and other adaptations in the Swedish banking sector should not exceed 5 billion kronor. Implementation costs outside the banking sector should be added... These costs amount to several billion kronor but are probably less, and of quite another magnitude, than the annual savings due to currency transactions...' *SOU 1996*: 158, p. 72.
27. *Sydsvenska Dagbladet*, 6 July 2003.
28. Ådahl and Eklund, *Allt om EMU*, p. 92.
29. *Ibid.*
30. 'Floating krona a risk for Sweden', *Dagens Nyheter*, 27 April 2003. Why 'an action of preparedness' should be necessary was made clear by Lindbeck one month before the previous referendum, about membership in the EU: 'Assar Lindbeck alarms about EU's monetary union: "Sweden in danger of

suffering a catastrophe of unemployment"', according to *Arbetet*, 13 October 1994.
31. 'We will agree on an EMU buffer', *Dagens Nyheter*, 13 July 2003.
32. R. Ohlsson, 'Det svenska välfärdssamhällets framväxt – tacka kvinnorna för det', *Socialvetenskaplig tidskrift*, 1, 1995, pp. 4–25.
33. OECD, 'Basic structural statistics', *Main economic indicators*, December 2002.
34. 'Lysande utsikter om euron införs', news article in *Dagens Nyheter*, 3 June 2003.
35. ECB, *Annual Report 2002*, p. 226.
36. Data about the *Riksbanken* from its *Annual Reports*.
37. Göran Persson in speeches and debates 1997, according to *Sydsvenska Dagbladet*, 6 July 2003.
38. Ådahl and Eklund, *Allt om EMU*, p. 82.
39. Reuters, 30 June 2003. Towards the end of the electoral campaign the exchange rate came into focus through a remarkable twist: Prime Minister Persson said the adoption of the euro might be delayed even with a 'Yes', if when negotiating the exchange rate Sweden would be given an 'impudent offer', according to *Aftonbladet*, 30 August 2003.

2

Borders Matter: Why the Euro is a Mistake and Why it will Fail

Arjo Klamer

Once the euro is a fact, the discussion subsides. The pragmatic interest of making it work comes to prevail. A critic is then made to feel like an unconstructive spoiler of the game. The train has to go on. There is no alternative (an expression that goes by the name of TINA). There is no way back. But what if the foundations of the edifice that has to keep the euro afloat are weak and shaky? What if a shock wave of some kind or another might be able to bring this entire edifice down? It would be something to reckon with. Scientists, at least, have the responsibility to point out the foundational weaknesses, and have to repeat their warnings whether those in power are willing to listen or not. These very doubts should encourage politicians to work on the foundations as well as on routes of escape. And those who consider getting into the building of the euro may recoil when they acknowledge the weakness of the foundations of the EMU.

The foundational criticism was to no avail when the Dutch cabinet and parliament faced the euro decision. The outcome of that decision had been a foregone conclusion. It did not matter that it lacked strong economic arguments, that many, including a group of 100 prominent economists, were opposed. It did not matter that the adoption of a common currency was generally deemed to be risky, that Dutch society stood to lose. It did not matter that many, including the Minister of Finance, agreed that the Dutch would enter at too low a rate, with the danger of being under-priced and facing higher inflation as a consequence. It did not matter that some warned against the possibility of money illusion and great confusion (especially among older people) about the new currency and an increased risk of being cheated over prices. The train had to move on, as European logic dictates. The euro was the necessary next step in the process towards a closer union. The Dutch acquiesced.

In the meantime, money illusion has plagued the Dutch. Even one and a half years after the introduction of the euro, people have not adjusted to the new currency. Many continue to calculate their income, prices and the value of real estate in guilders. Prices of flowers (a Dutch essential), groceries, beer, coffee, sandwiches, restaurant meals have shot up, causing great unrest and frustration. Small retailers, in particular, have tried to benefit from the transition. Fear of crashing pension systems in fellow euro countries add to the ill feeling about the euro. The advantage of being able to use the euro on vacation in France or Italy is only a minor compensation. But all these problems, no matter how real they are, remain superficial. The real problems go deeper; they concern the very foundations of the construction that has to support the euro.

The argumentation, therefore, takes us beyond the strictly economic domain. Although it is in the interest of economists and, as it turns out, politicians to stick to an economic argumentation, a more complete assessment requires the inclusion of the political, social and cultural dimensions. Let me show how, and why this line of argumentation leads to the conclusion that the euro has to fail.

The argument begins with the acknowledgement of the two sides of the coin

A coin has two sides. One side shows a number and stands for its value in traffic. That is the value that usually receives most attention. For wouldn't it be easy if the number 1 on a coin would stand for the same value anywhere, in Sweden, the Netherlands, the US, China, Mali, that is, anywhere? In that case the same coin would be legal tender the world over. There would be no costs of exchange, no variable exchange rates with the risks that they involve. Such a currency we could coin the uno. Many arguments in favour of the euro are actually arguments in favour of a *uno*. When elimination of transaction costs and the risks of flexible exchange rates are the objectives, the euro is only an intermediate solution on the way to the uno.

A lot can be said in favour of a common currency, be it the euro or the uno. The protagonists will repeat the mostly economic arguments over and over again. They will highlight economic gains in terms of lower costs, more trade and higher economic growth. But even when we stick to the economics, a lot can also be said against a common currency (see also the other chapters in this volume). The elimination of exchange rates implies the loss of prices, and with those a mechanism to accommodate asymmetric shocks to the system and to allow for relatively easy and quick readjustments. The political authorities in the euro area now lack the instruments with which to conduct macroeconomic policies. They not only lost the exchange rate as an instrument but also the interest rate and, due to the Stability Pact, the government budget to some extent (since they are not allowed to run up a deficit of more than 3 per cent of GDP). A few years after fighting to get the Stability Pact as part of the euro deal, Germany itself is forced to violate the Pact. In 2003 and 2004 Germany had to run up deficits in excess of 3 per cent of its GDP in order to deal with its recession.

There is, furthermore, a great deal of uncertainty about how the euro countries should respond in the case of one of them being in serious financial troubles. Should countries take care of themselves – as is suggested by the political leadership – or does the common currency compel the other euro countries to bail out their weaker members in order to bolster the external value of the euro?

Critics also have questioned the economic gains that are attributed to the euro. The lacklustre performance of the euro countries after the introduction of the euro bears out these doubts. When advocates retort that slow economic growth is due to world-wide slackness, they are subdued by pointing at the UK, Denmark, Norway and Sweden, all of which have done relatively well without the euro.

Regardless of what side they support, economic arguments are never conclusive. History shows that the protagonists of the euro cannot be right all the time under any circumstances. Monetary regimes do not last indefinitely. Gold standards, regimes of fixed exchange rates and common currency areas – they all have a limited life span. Therefore it is not unthinkable that the euro will fail. How could it not, given what history tells us. Then again, once upon a time the dollar, the German mark and the Italian lire were introduced as a common currency and were sustained. Only a free political decision could end the reigns of the lire and the mark. The dollar keeps going.

So why do some monetary arrangements last whereas most others have a limited life span?

An answer may be found by looking at the other side of the coin. That side shows a symbol that stands for the community that has issued it and in which it is supposed to circulate. The symbol usually is the head of the monarch if there is one, or a sign that stands for the nation. With all the talk about the economic aspects of the coin, people are inclined to ignore this side and to think that a national community does not matter and that the coin can function without it. Yet, it can't.

A coin needs to be managed. A currency needs to be embedded in a complex institutional framework. There is the need for a central bank that manages the money supply, insofar as it is capable of doing so, and oversees the other money-creating institutions, the banks. A central political authority is required to manage the national house-hold, including its expenditures, the tax system and the resultant government deficit. A government that is forcing its central bank to print money in order to finance its expenses will undermine the trust in the national currency. That is why the independence of the central bank is deemed so important. But it takes a good government to grant and secure such independence.

Trust is crucial for a monetary system based on fiduciary money. Without it the system will collapse in a spiral of ever-increasing infla-tion and decreasing exchange rates. There is more. Conflicts between employers and trade unions can drive up wages and prices leaving a central bank powerless. It can step up the brake but it will not be able to bring the increasing inflation to a halt unless it gets the co-operation of the other parties involved. Monetary systems can also succumb when regional differences become untenable, and that can happen when external shocks impact the regions of the common currency area differently. Only a concerted effort of monetary, and especially political, authorities can avert such a collapse.

The other side of the coin, therefore, points at the need for a strong political system to guarantee the durability of a monetary system. History tells us time and again that durable currencies came about only after the establishment of a strong political union, or at least, a political entity with a strong and dominant political centre. The fact that the United States of America were ready for one single dollar several decades after they had fought one of the bloodiest wars ever to secure the continuance of their federation has shown that all this can happen. The German mark came about thanks to the strong leadership of Prussia. We do not know of any common currency areas that endured decentred and unstable political systems.

The drafters of the Treaty of Maastricht were fully aware of the importance of a strong political union as the basis for their monetary union. They were therefore intent on measures that would move the political European union towards a federal construction. Many federal institutions were already in place, like the European parliament, the European Commission and the European court. More centralization was required in order to unify economic and also foreign policies (although the latter issue was not discussed openly). When the political measures ran into formidable opposition, Jacques Delors and the then presiding Dutch prime minister (Ruud Lubbers) decided to move ahead with the monetary union anyway. The presumption was that once the monetary union was a fact, a kind of federal construction, or at least a closer political union, would have to follow in order to make the monetary union work. Thus, the wagon was put in front of the horse. It was an experiment. No politician dared to face the question of what the consequences would be of failure, or of what would happen if a strong political union did not come about. The train had to go on. TINA.

Accordingly, a strong political union appears to be a condition for the durable success of a monetary union. A political union exists by virtue of borders. It is only by drawing borders that its rulers know who are their subjects or fellow-citizens. The border cordons off those who are able to vote, have to pay taxes and are the beneficiaries of the welfare system. The border marks the political space with its citizens and the coverage of relevant political news. (Political squabbles and events are relevant till the border; only a few events make their way across. Belgians are not interested in the political news of the Netherlands and the Dutch have no need for news about Belgian political stuff.)

What, then, are good borders? Where should they be drawn? Does the European Union do well by drawing them ever larger? By having ever more countries join to union to widen its borders? Or is the European Union getting too big for its own good? The questions are important when we consider the viability of the euro. Its durability requires a vital political entity. If the borders are being drawn too wide, too far away, the political union is doomed to unravel. And the unravelling will lead to the failure of the euro.

The issue of borders

Raising the issue of borders is touchy nowadays. We are taught to think of a borderless world. The breaking down of borders is believed to be a good thing. Borders are under attack everywhere. They have to disappear where they separate the high arts from low arts and one scientific discipline from the other. They vanish in the network society that thinkers like Manuel Castells imagine to be our future.[1] They fade away with the decline of the nation states. The ideal of a borderless world motivates the gradual erasure of the European nation states to have them dissolve in something bigger.

In my science, that of economics, borders have only a negative connotation. Markets are, in principle, borderless. Ideal markets are global allowing individuals all over the world to trade with whomever, wherever. Borders are only obstacles, hindering free trade. An entire subdiscipline, that of international economics, focuses on the problems and issues that borders introduce. The presumption is that where markets are allowed to function unhindered, borders will disappear. When the trading across a border intensifies, when people just as easily choose an employer on the other side, when capital roams freely in search of the best return, borders will loose their function. We see it with dialects: they disappear when people seek a common language to facilitate their economic interactions. At any rate, open markets, free trade, are presented as the condition for maximal welfare. If it were up to economists, all countries would open their borders for foreign trade. Everybody would be better off, including the poor in the Third World. To them globalization, the world market, the multi- or transnationals and the network society rule the economic imagination.

Even so borders are everywhere. Some are stronger and more hermetic than others. But there they are, separating the domain of one family from another, marking the boundaries of an organization, defining city limits and separating political entities from each other. Why are they there? What functions do they serve?

The *raison d'être* of border

Although there are economic theories to explain the disappearance of borders and the diminishing powers of national states, I do not know of any economic theory that explains why borders exist and why they are where they are. Might there be economic reasons why the Netherlands maintains borders with Belgium and Canadians insist on the maintenance of borders with the US?

Borders serve, first of all, a social purpose. Families need to draw borders to mark their space. These borders are physical and imaginary. They appear in the form of fences, walls, closed doors and the like, but also in institutions like privacy, marriage, divorce, hospitality. It is only possible to invite people into one's house when something prevents people from wandering in. The institutions of marriage and divorce indicate how serious people are about their personal borders, and how emotional the union and separation of two personal domains are.

Borders also serve economic purposes. The idea of the network society may suggest that individuals interact freely, moving in and out at will, forming numerous connections with other individuals. In reality, we continue to observe clusterings, the formation of groups, the survival of organizations like businesses. The reason is, as Ronald Coase showed back in 1937, that free transactions can be costly.[2] Setting up a new connection, and sustaining it, can be costly. One has to find the right individual and negotiate a deal while uncertain about the credentials of the other. That's why people organize themselves and move into buildings under one label, the name of their company. Such an organization saves on transaction costs, but it also allows for specific forms of governance. Companies enable the formation of hierarchical decision procedures, the appeal to loyalty. Companies facilitate the development of a corporate culture, a trade mark and other aspects with which the people of that company distinguish themselves from other companies. This is not to say that companies are to be preferred over networks. I just observe that people continue to operate in groups. And they need to draw borders in order to do so.

People form groups to cope with the uncertainty that they face. At least, this is a point that Siegwart Lundenberg makes in his survey of theories of the group.[3] The group forms a common frame of reference and a collective consciousness and functions by virtue of various interdependencies. Families hold together because of a sense of mutual responsibility, a common history, shared tasks (like care for the children). Groups hold together as long as they produce shared goods, like a sense of membership, and values, like a sense of responsibility, care and mutual affection (and hatred?).

Borders serve political purposes, too. Just like borders mark a company, borders mark a nation state and its political system. Without borders there would not be a democracy; without borders a welfare state would quickly perish. The borders of a country define its political space. And that space determines who are the citizens, which responsibilities they have and which rights they derive from dwelling within those borders. The citizens are expected to make sacrifices by paying taxes to finance internal affairs and to support fellow citizens in need of support. They may even collect money to give to citizens that dwell within other borders – development aid as it is called. Borders make the 'imagined communities', as Anderson called nations, concrete.[4]

Border conflicts underscore the importance of borders. People are willing to sacrifice their lives defending borders, or crossing them. The enforcing of borders may run into serious problems, as we have witnessed in Africa and the Middle East. Borders drawn badly cause extended conflicts and wars.

Borders are far from fixed. They get redrawn all the time. The European Union, for example, is extending its borders by allowing more and more member countries in. The breaking up of the Soviet Union and Yugoslavia meant the contraction of all kinds of borders. While national borders are getting murkier, regional and city borders are getting more pronounced. Borders are dynamic things.

The positive values of nation states and nationalism

Nation states have not always been. As a matter of fact, national borders came about only during the last few centuries. Their construction has worked better in Europe than it has in the Middle East and Africa. Benedict Anderson argues that the rise of the modern state was a response to the decline of religion and the influence of sacred texts and language. Where people of all kinds of tribes and ethnicities share the same religion and the same texts, they are less in need of national borders. In the Middle Ages people of Western

Europe had one God, read one Bible and obeyed one Church with the pope as its leader. With the fading of Latin, the rise of science, and the discovery of new territory, the grip of the Church loosened and people were in need of other contexts to produce the necessary common goods. Monarchies made up for some of this, but they, too, had to cede to the modern national state, based on democratic principles. The important point to be stressed here is that people need to be able to imagine community. In the words of Anderson:

> In an age when it is so common for progressive, cosmopolitan intellectuals (particularly in Europe?) to insist on the near-pathological character of nationalism, its roots in fear and hatred of the Other, and its affinities with racism, it is useful to remind ourselves that nations inspire love, and often profoundly self-sacrificing love. The cultural products of nationalism – poetry, prose fiction, music, plastic arts – show this love very clearly in thousands of different forms and styles.[5]

Anderson refers here to the phenomenon that people are willing to sacrifice their lives for country but would not even think of doing so much if their profession or their firm was to be threatened.

Big versus small

One of the few economists who has looked into the bordering of nations is Alberto Alesina. In collaboration with various other scholars he has tried to develop a theory that accounts for borders getting drawn larger or smaller.[6] The question is: which factors account for the size of nations? He subsequently subjected his models to empirical tests. A full account of his argument will take us too far away from our argumentation. The gist may suffice.

Nations become big for all kinds of reasons. Power is one. Larger countries usually have more political weight in the international arena. Size, however, does not guarantee power as Brazil, India and the like show. Other important reasons are economic. Enlargement of the nation saves costs on the public provisions because of economies of scale. Public expenditures on goods like defence, safety, the judicial system and a monetary system will go down per head of the population. Tax collection becomes relatively cheaper. Large nations can undertake large infrastructural projects; large nations can absorb shocks more easily and have the ability to reduce regional differences by redistribution of funds. Large nations also imply large domestic markets. This latter factor is especially important when farmers and industrialists face trade barriers all around. A large nation can eliminate these barriers within its own domain and so allow free exchange.

All these reasons motivated the founding fathers of the United States of America. They saw the power, the savings and the benefits of a larger domestic market. At their time they seemed to be right. Similar arguments appear to propel the eurocrats towards an ever greater and closer union. We hear arguments for the need for a countervailing power *vis-à-vis* the US, about economies of scale, about more effective policies towards the environment, migration and such issues, and, of course, about the large European market that will be even larger than the American one.

As with everything, growing larger has also its disadvantages. The political system may become more unwieldy. The population may become too heterogeneous to allow for a communal feeling. Solidarity will wane as a consequence. Democratic procedures may get thwarted or run into apathy. Individual citizens may find it more difficult to identify with the rulers of the country, or will find the distance to the corridors of power too great. Larger nations also tend to pay a price for their power. American citizens now contribute more than three times to their 'defence' forces than their German and French counterparts. American soldiers have to sacrifice their lives for their country whereas the soldiers of small countries remain unexposed. These negatives are among the reasons why nations can become smaller.

Accordingly, groups of citizens may want to secede from large nations to reinforce their identity, to revitalize their democracy and to secure their social welfare (avoiding a drain of resources to other parts of the large country or the imposition of watered-down provisions). The advantage of being smaller is greater homogeneity. The chance of reaching agreement on complicated matters is increased. The political system becomes more flexible and democratic, and more attention goes to education, care and welfare. Smaller, more homogeneous nations have a better chance for a developed and advanced civil society (think of political parties, societies, clubs, non-profit organizations and the like) than a larger nation. And a developed and advanced civil society is critical for a well-functioning democracy as Robert Putnam has showed.[7] These are political and social advantages to smaller nations.

There are also economic advantages to being small. As the new economic theories of Paul Krugman, among others, indicate, economic efficiency benefits from the clustering of similar enterprises in a geographical space. Businesses do better in the proximity of other businesses of the same kind. Accordingly, entertainment industries cluster in Hollywood, IT businesses in Silicon Valley and flower businesses in Holland. When clusters become strong they may desire special policies and this will stimulate the drive for political independence.

More importantly, the advantage of large domestic markets disappears with the removal of protectionist barriers. Dutch flower producers can now freely sell their flowers all over the world. They do not need the formation of a large internal market. (Merchants do not stand to benefit anyway from such a market as they are good at dealing with protectionist barriers. Merchants go where the opportunities are.) You would expect that economies become smaller when trade becomes more liberal.

And that is precisely what Alesina finds. Whereas there were 74 countries in 1946, there are now 191 or 192 countries (depending on whether the Vatican counts as a country or not). Most of these countries are small. Eighty-seven countries have fewer than 5 million inhabitants. Between the two world wars the number of countries had stagnated. In the century before the number had declined. The explosion of countries after World War II is related to the end of the colonization, of course, and the demise of the Soviet empire. But note that all these new, and usually small, nations saw a chance in the liberal climate of the post-war period. They saw a chance to cut the tie with their colonial ruler or mighty Russia and go on their own. (What most of these countries did first, incidentally, was adopt their own currency!) As Alesina concludes, economic integration leads to political 'disintegration'.

Furthermore, Alesina shows that, overall, small economies do better economically than large economies. The US is the big exception. Otherwise small economies such as Norway, Sweden, the Netherlands, Switzerland, Singapore and Kuwait do best. Sure, some benefit from their natural resources. But most of them also excel on other counts, like the vitality of their democracies, the health of their welfare system and the overall happiness of their people. When you consider all these data, you are led to wonder why the European leaders want to become so big together so desperately. The European move to enlargement, towards an ever-larger internal market, is contrary to what we see elsewhere in the world.

Alesina, however, argues that Europe is less of an anomaly than it seems. Although the apparent trend is towards a large political union, federalized in some form or another, the result will be strengthened and more autonomous regions. The nations of Spain, Italy, the UK and Germany will disintegrate as the regions of Wales, Scotland, the Basque country and the various states that make up Germany and Northern Italy assert themselves as independent political entities. So big Europe will end up with more small economies than when it started. All these small economies will have to co-operate on all kinds of issues but will develop their own internal democracies and welfare systems.

Instability

Opposition towards an ever closer European union, therefore, might focus on the costs in terms of a loss in democratic and social values. The democratic deficit continues to haunt the European experiment. Each time political leaders in Europe target the deficit and each time they come up short. The European convention had to generate a public debate and became a debate in public instead. Citizens continue to be indifferent towards Europe. Or they proclaim themselves Europeans without a clue as to what that means. No politician dares to be serious about a European tax, afraid that the populace will turn against Europe. In the meantime, European institutions garner more power. While the European parliament works in isolation, national parliaments are left out in the cold.

The weakness of this edifice is the political construction. Much has to be expected of the political efficacy of the European Union. A common currency adds to its political responsibilities. But the edifice is weak and shaky. Too much depends on the good will of the large members, too much is determined by means of compromises, too often one or another member has to pay too high a price for a compromise. The question is how long this constellation of old countries with long and often problematic histories will hold. Who would have expected that the union that Tito had forged between the Balkan countries would fall apart? Weren't these countries economically interdependent? Hadn't the various ethnic groups intermingled? And how about the Soviet empire? The latter could absorb one shock wave after another, but in the end it gave in. Such an artificial construction does not hold. The European construction is artificial, too. Why would it hold where all other such constructions have failed?

Our experiment is unique, the eurocrats insist. Maybe it is. Maybe this Europe will be first, with other similar constructions to follow in Latin America and Asia. But it is so unlikely.

All kinds of shocks can threaten the shaky cohesion of this Europe. One genre is economic. Nobody knows whether the EMU will withstand a major financial crisis. It will be especially difficult when the pain is distributed unevenly. Say the Germans and Spaniards bear the brunt of the burden. How willing will they be to co-operate on tough policy decisions? Will France accept a penalty that it gets because of the conditions of the Stability Pact? How will the French react? What if they have to vote on new constitutional rules? A 'No' vote from tiny Luxemburg is enough to halt the political process in the European Union. Decisions can be forced with the usual blackmail: 'if you do not comply, the political union is in danger and you do not want to be responsible for its demise, do you?' How long can the political leaders keep up this game? This Europe with its 25 more or less autonomous members is becoming a game-theoretic nightmare with no equilibrium solution in sight.

The real shock is more likely to be political or social. Citizens may be up in arms when they find that something that is important to them is taken away or abolished by the EU, when they cannot keep their cattle, grow their cheese, hold on to their liberal drug laws, or they are forced to side against a friend in an international conflict. Each shock could mean the end. In the beginning compromises will be found, ill-feelings are suppressed. But the anger and frustration will build up to erupt when a new shock hits.

The common currency stands little chance. It could succumb for all kinds of reasons. The European Central Bank may prove to be politically powerless to control inflationary forces in member countries. Strong national banks usually owe their power to their credibility in national policies. When Duisenberg, then president of the European

Central Bank, waved his finger as the president of the Dutch Central bank and warned against high demands by the labour union, everybody, including the Dutch labour unions, paid attention. But would they respond if a Frenchman waved his finger? A central bank needs the support of national political bodies and there is no guarantee that it will have that support. When nations want to conduct their own policies to counter negative economic shocks, they may end up having a conflict not only with the European Central Bank and the European Commission but also with each other. Imagine if Germany decided to withdraw from the euro and return to the mark. The Dutch would have to follow. No protagonist wants to consider the possibility of this happening. The desire to believe that the euro will last forever is so strong that it becomes just that, a belief, and a romantic belief at that.

Maybe this view is too pessimistic. Maybe it is realistic.

Conclusion

TINA? Is there no other alternative? Returning to the argumentation of Alesina, small economies and manageable democracies are something to look forward to. They will do better not only democratically and socially but also economically. An ever-larger European Union will most likely not lead us to a better democracy and, as it looks now, does not promise better and more generous social policies. A larger European Union will have difficulties adjusting its policies to work towards a more dynamic, up-to-date economy. Small is better.

Even so, it is important to stress the gains made with the European Union. Because of a more liberal trade regime, because of the elimination of barriers between economies, small economies have better chances. Economic integration has been good overall. To counter the tendency of the closing of an ever closer European Union, the push has to be for international bodies that invite all relevant stakeholders to the table. Such bodies have to be much less stringent in allowing new members to take part in their deliberations than the European councils are now. The environment does not stop at the border with Bulgaria, and the problem of immigration involves the regions of origin. Foreign affairs are international and so are better dealt with in truly international bodies.

There are alternatives. Once such alternatives can be imagined, the construction with a common currency appears far-fetched and contra-productive. European countries do better by being small, and thus by being open and by collaborating intensely with each other. They may opt for a common currency. Then again, they may prefer to have their own.

Notes

1. M. Castells, *The Rise of the Network Society*, Oxford: Basil Blackwell, 1996.
2. R.H. Coase, 'The Nature of the Firm', *Economica*, vol. 2–4 (issue 16), 1937, pp. 386–405.
3. S. Lundenberg, 'Grounding Groups in Theory: Functional, Cognitive, and Structural Interdependencies', *Advances in Group Processes*, 14, 1997, pp. 281–331.
4. B. Anderson, *Imagined Communities*, London: Verso, 1991 (1983).
5. *Ibid.*, p. 141.
6. A. Alesina and E. Spolaore, 'On the Number and Size of Nations', *Quarterly Journal of Economics*, 112 (November 1997), pp. 1027–56.
7. R. Putnam, *Making Democracy Work*, Princeton: Princeton University Press, 1994.

3
The Stability Pact:
A Macroeconomic Straitjacket!

Jesper Jespersen

Introduction

From the theory of Optimal Currency Areas (OCA) we know that the European Monetary Union (EMU) is certainly not an OCA. This observation implies that on the one hand the member countries will have a macroeconomic development that differs, but have, due to membership of the EMU, got much limited room for manoeuvre for pursuing an independent macroeconomic policy.

The pivotal element of the EMU is the common currency adopted by all the participating countries. By accepting a common currency the individual countries have definitively cut themselves off from pursuing an independent exchange rate and monetary policy. If the participating countries experience different rates of inflation or employment in the future, membership of the EMU reduces dramatically the political room for manoeuvre. Fiscal policy is the only policy instrument left to the member countries for individual demand management policies. But even fiscal policy is restricted through the acceptance of the Stability and Growth Pact (SGP). This Pact states that the public sector borrowing requirement never exceeds 3 per cent of the GDP and, furthermore, requires that any country should actively adjust the budget each year in an attempt to secure that any deficit on the public sector accounts vanishes within two to three years. It is the Commission that ensures that these constraints are respected by the member states and can propose that those countries that do not conform to the requirements are asked to pay a fine, which in severe cases can amount to ½ per cent of GDP.

The increasing unemployment in Germany and France has accentuated the feasibility of the SGP and renewed the debate of its relevance for the proper functioning of the EMU. The chairman of the Commission, Romano Prodi, made the most outspoken comment on that dilemma. In an interview with the French newspaper *Le Monde* in October 2002,[1] he called the very rigid rules of the SGP 'stupid' – plain talk, certainly. And that statement was not a slip of the tongue; he knows what he is talking about, having previously been a professor of economics at the University of Bologna. Of course, Mr Prodi was immediately corrected by the defenders of the pan-European ideas, who, instead, could have benefited from listening to someone who is committed to Europe, but has kept an independent mind. He is sincerely worried about the consequences of strict adherence to the words of the SGP by the European Council. If no exceptions can be allowed he fears that there will an increased risk of Europe experiencing a prolonged period of high unemployment. In that case it would just be a kind of repetition of the 1990s where a number of the potential EMU countries went through a period of low growth and high unemployment when they adapted to the severe criteria of convergence built into the Treaty of Maastricht. That development contributed significantly to the high rate of unemployment, especially in Germany.

The Stability Pact increases unemployment[2]

The SGP was agreed upon by the 15 EU member states in 1997 as a supplement to the original EMU text. Within the Treaty of Maastricht it was only decided what conditions a country should fulfil to get access to the EMU; no rules of conduct after entry has been permitted were established. In many ways the very strict entry conditions, the so-called convergence criteria, were originally intended to transform the economic performance of any potential member country into a low-inflation, low-budget-deficit economy. The main convergence criterion was related to the size of the budget deficit. It had to be smaller than 3 per cent of GDP; but suddenly the Germans realized that some countries were able to dress up their budget in that specific year. Hence, to ensure that the improvement of the budget was not just a one off, the German minister of finance asked his colleagues to agree on a permanent reduction of the budget deficit.

It was never clearly expressed why it is so important that member states balance their public books; but the immediate consequence was that the strict fiscal policy which had ruled the 1990s was prolonged into the next century. This was especially so because the SGP put an upper limit to the size of the budget deficit without regard to the business cycle situation. In addition, it requires the 'deficit countries' to remove the deficit within a time horizon of two to three years without any consideration of the consequences for growth and employment. In fact, the SGP is more restrictive than the original convergence criteria. The EMU countries were in the middle of this adjustment process when they were hit by the international depression in the year 2000. Of course, the individual European countries were hit differently, but the paradox of the SGP is that the harder a country is hit the more it is forced to restrict its fiscal policy. That has a damaging effect on the country itself but also has contagious consequences for the neighbouring countries. Thus, a vicious cycle is started within the EMU countries which now have no macroeconomic policy instruments left to be used at their own discretion.

The Stability Pact has a built-in misperception of macroeconomic theory[3]

The requirements with regard to the public sector budget within the SGP can be presented the following way:

1. A *sound budget*, in the sense of a balanced budget or even a surplus for a full business cycle. That is the main requirement which should always guide the fiscal policy.
2. A *stable budget*, in the sense that the deficit – except for the case of a true depression – must not exceed 3 per cent of GDP.
3. Furthermore the Commission contemplated adding one more requirement, namely that the member states make the public budget *sustainable*, in the sense that the surplus should be large enough to cover the increased expenses in the future caused by the demographical changes.

The above-listed three conditions could, from an immediate reading, sound quite reasonable, if one was to consider the economic strategy of a single household. Then they could be translated in the following way: 1. adjust current income to current expenses; 2. in extraordinary circumstances (sickness, unemployment etc.) a temporary, but minor deficit is accepted – but plans of how to redress it have to be put forward; and 3. don't forget to save for your old age. This is the economic behaviour expected by a *bonus pater familias*. Exactly for that reason it is very easy to argue in a convincing way that what is sound economics for an individual household should also hold true for public sector policy? Furthermore, it is an argument that is pretty straightforward to present in a political debate with ordinary people, because it has a direct appeal to 'common sense'.

The only problem with the household argument is that it does not apply in the macroeconomic context. And that is precisely what separates arguments related to the entire public sector from microeconomic reasoning. In fact, any serious macroeconomist knows that one of the main functional differences between a single household or a firm and the public sector is that individuals have to balance their books, but the aim of the government should be to balance the entire domestic economy. When an unconditioned parallel is drawn from microeconomic argument to macroeconomic conclusions there is an obvious risk of committing the so-called theoretical 'fallacy of composition'. You have to be a trained macroeconomist to know these theoretical arguments; but if you do have this in-depth understanding and have geniune interests at heart – like Romano Prodi – then you are not in doubt when you are confronted with such a fallacious argument that micro- and macroeconomic reasoning leads to the same conclusions.

The private and the public sectors cannot be analyzed separately

The father of macroeconomic theory is John Maynard Keynes. Within his seminal text *The General Theory of Employment, Interest and Money* (1936) he demonstrated that the essence of macroeconomic theory is to understand how the collective actions of numerous consuming households and investing firms were transformed into *effective demand for goods and services* which determines the level of activity in society. One of his main conclusions was that there is no automatic mechanism within a modern market economy that ensures that the level of activity generated by the private sector should correspond to anything similar to full employment or full-capacity utilization. Keynes had observed in the inter-war period that 'an outstanding characteristic of the economic system in which we live is its capability of remaining in a chronic condition of sub-normal activity for a considerable period without any marked tendency either towards recovery or towards complete collapse'.[4]

Even in case of perfect competition ruling in any single market there will be no guarantee that the economy as a whole would generate stable growth with full employment. The assumption of perfect competition might secure a fairly good co-ordination in any single market, but does not guarantee a perfect interaction between all the markets which constitute the entire macroeconomic system. One of the consequences of this lack of macro co-ordination is that private savings often run ahead of real investments undertaken by firms, making the macroeconomic under-perform and deviate from anything like full employment. In fact, in a historical period where, demographically, society is growing older there could easily be a rather substantial tendency towards over-saving, because *bonus pater familias* wants to save for his old age, which is approaching quite quickly.

Keynes made the point that within a modern industrial society the major part of household savings go into financial assets. These decisions with regard to saving are made independent of the prospect of making profitable real investments. The macroeconomic problem is that saving is an act of not consuming, that is, of reducing the effective demand for goods and services and by that creating unemployment. If real investment is lagging behind savings there is a permanent gap between effective demand and the output capacity that creates the 'condition of sub-normal activity' which characterized the inter-war period *and* European economy since the early 1980s. This is the theoretical background against which Keynes concluded that the state had a moral obligation to secure a better match between saving and investment through increased public investment in periods of over-saving in the private sector. Keynes made this recommendation not because he loved state intervention (he was, in fact, a member of the Liberal Party), but because his macroeconomic theory told him that only the state could implement the overall demand management policy that was (and still is) needed to secure stable growth and full employment.

Furthermore, Keynes would have much preferred an active monetary policy than fiscal policy to match private savings and real investments.[5] But at his time monetary policy was blocked by a very conservative policy by the Bank of England. Today monetary policy within the EMU is constrained by an anti-inflation bias in the policy of the European Central Bank (ECB).

From this macroeconomic point of view it is not meaningful to set up specific conditions with regard to the size and development of the public sector borrowing requirement, because the budget of the public sector is a mirror image of behaviour within the private sector. Any requirement concerning a balanced public budget is equivalent to requiring a balance between savings and real investment within the private sector. If the government of an EMU country is forced to reduce its deficit by, say, 1 per cent of GDP, the Commission in Brussels could equally have required the private sector to reduce its excess savings (its budget surplus) by 1 per cent. Private savings are made out of current income. Hence, private savings are reduced through a reduction of current income, which is equal to asking the private sector to decrease its economic activity, that is, reduce economic growth, as a consequence of the Stability and Growth Pact!

This simple definition of the important macroeconomic relationship between the public and the private sector, and by that between the public sector budget and growth and employment, seems much too often to be overlooked. An unfortunate, but not very exceptional statement about the (lack of) correlation between economic performance and the SGP states:

> The fall-off of the economic growth in the year 2002 together with the huge budget problems that Germany and France experience is a good illustration of the intention behind the Stability and Growth Pact. Because, if these countries had acted in accordance with the aim of the Pact and adjusted the budget to the requirement of 'near to balance' during the period 1999–2001, where the growth was favourable, then, today, they would have had no problems with the 3 per cent upper limit of the budget deficit.[6]

The above argument seems to overlook the fact that a fiscal restriction in 1999–2001 would have made the growth less favourable and unemployment in that period even higher. There is no convincing argument that higher unemployment should be preferred to a smaller budget deficit, in sofar as it is just mirroring over-saving in the private sector. Furthermore, the arbitrary limit of 3 per cent is not even debated it is just taken for granted, which makes the argument even less persuasive.

The situation is compounded by the fact that no differentiation is made in the requirements of the SGP between current public expenditure and public investment. No private firm could ever dream about financing its real investment entirely from current income. Long-term real investment should be financed by borrowing, especially in a period where the private sector is having an excess of financial savings. In other words it is not sound budget policy to ask the public sector to balance its current and capital accounts independent of how the private sector is behaving.

There seem to be strong theoretical arguments for revising the SGP with regard to the arbitrary limit of 3 per cent and excluding public real investment as a requirement of a balanced budget. Furthermore, the relationship between the public sector borrowing requirements and unemployment has to be analyzed more thoroughly.

The role of automatic budget stabilizers – the case of Sweden

It is well known that in modern welfare states there is a rather strong relationship between the public sector current income and expenses and economic growth. As soon as the growth process peters out tax revenues fall behind and expenditures exceed the figures in the budget which are based on the expectation of 'normal' growth. The so-called automatic stabilizers of the public sector budget cause this deviation of the actual figures from the planned one. They have the beneficial effect of reducing the up- and downswings of the business cycle; but at the price of larger fluctuations in the public sector budget. The more extensive the organization of the welfare system, the larger the automatic stabilizers. Hence, there will be a substantial difference between the Scandinavian welfare states and the much more limited British one, making the size of the automatic stabilizers very different. From this perspective the fixed limit of 3 per cent, which is similar for all countries, becomes even more arbitrary, because some countries (especially the Scandinavian, see Figure 3.1) are more exposed to large fluctuations in the public budget when the growth process weakens than, for instance, Great Britain.

The OECD has made a number of studies of the relationship between budget deficit and the development in growth and unemployment in European countries. Historically it has been more the rule than the exception that the European countries had a deficit exceeding 3 per cent when the trough of the business cycle was passed due to the functioning of the automatic stabilizers. Although these historical facts were well known in 1997 it was argued that the European economies would undergo substantial changes in their transition to the EMU and that in the future they would perform differently and be more stable. In that case, the fluctuations in the budget caused by the automatic stabilizers would have been correspondingly reduced.

Despite a number of proposals from the Commission in Brussels to scale down the welfare state, the correlation between the business cycle and the budget is unchanged in EMU countries. Hence, within two years of the launching of the euro in 1999 the first country was to break the conditions of the SGP. Portugal had a deficit in 2001 of more than 4 per cent of GDP. The following year Germany followed suit, and in 2003 it was the French budget that was hit by the weakening of economic growth. The attitude in Brussels towards these 'excessive' budget deficits was somewhat different. Portugal was forced to correct the deficit within one year by reductions in public expenditures and sales of public real assets. However, the attitude towards Germany and France was more relaxed and neither of these countries are expected to bring the deficit within the 3 per cent limit before 2005. This seemingly more lax attitude towards the bigger countries should not be interpreted as a renouncement on the SGP. Both countries have made a number a fiscal restraints which add up to a more restrictive fiscal policy than they would have pursued without the close and persistent examinations following the procedure of the SGP. This has caused the rate of unemployment to continue its upward trend for more than two years.

There are strong theoretically grounded arguments, supported by empirical evidence that the SGP is acting like a straightjacket on the EMU countries. It is not only the countries that have exceeded the limit that are constrained by a more restrictive fiscal policy than they would otherwise have undertaken. The other EU countries feel the constraints through lower exports to the German and French markets. It is only those countries that have kept a flowing exchange rate that are able to escape at least some of the deflationary effects, but at the expense of further depression on the EMU countries who are locked in by the common currency and, thus, by a fixed exchange rate.

Hence, it has become more and more obvious that the SGP in its actual shape is unnecessarily restrictive and unfair to the smaller countries and to those countries with the most extended welfare state. Within the Scandinavian countries, a 1 percentage point change in unemployment corresponds to a change in the budget deficit of nearly 1½ percentage points. This means that an increase in the rate of unemployment from, say, 5 per cent to 6 per cent would cause the public budget to go down by 1½ per cent of GDP. If Sweden was hit again by a recession of the same magnitude as the one the country experienced in 1991–3 the SGP would make the trough of the business cycle even deeper and more prolonged. When the deficit reached its peak in 1993 it had a magnitude of 12 per cent of GDP, which was even larger than the Danish in 1982. Should the deficit have been kept within the limit of 3 per cent, it would have required a reduction in the deficit of 9 percentage points. This would have made the rate of unemployment 6 percentage points higher and increased the rate

Figure 3.1   Sweden: unemployment and budget of the public sector

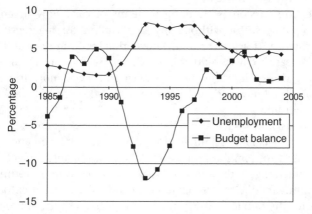

Source: OECD, *Economic Outlook*, vol. 2002/2, no. 72, December 2002, Annex table 21 and table 30.

of unemployment from 8 per cent to 14 per cent. Of course, the Swedish electorate would have asked why? Instead, Sweden changed its policies drastically and adopted a floating exchange rate in the autumn of 1992 which made the economy start to recover quite quickly.

A 'sustainable' budget

Fiscal discipline is not only about running sound public finances in the short to medium term. It also requires that public finances are sustainable in the long run, that is, that current budget policies do not lead to or risk causing future imbalances in breach of the Stability and Growth Pact requirements due to the budgetary effects of ageing population.[7]

When judging the budget of the member countries the Commission has proposed that, in addition to the *sound* and *stable* budget requirements discussed above, the budget should also be made *sustainable*. That means that the current budget should have a surplus which would enable the government to pay the higher expenses to old age pensioners with out increasing the taxes in the future. The idea behind this is the simple microeconomic argument that if a government accumulates financial wealth today then it can more easily cover its higher expenses in the future.

The Commission is thinking in terms of cash flow in and out of the public sector without any implications for macroeconomic performance. If a government knows that its future commitments will increase, why should it not start to save today to make the increase in expenditures more smooth and, even more important, to make the budget more resistant towards the risk of breaking the 3 per cent limit?

Previously, we have seen that the Commission defines a sound budget as a balanced budget that leaves the public financial debt unchanged in nominal terms. However, a sustainable budget would leave unchanged the present value of all future governmental commitments due to demographical changes. This is an extra argument for the public sector to run a surplus because the approaching demographical change will by itself increase the present value of the public obligations to future pensioners as a percentage of GDP.

Once again the Commission is falling prey to the 'fallacy of composition' when it argues that the government can reduce its future real commitments by increasing its financial savings today. If the relevant government were a single household this argument would be trivial, but it does not apply to the entire public sector. Commitments on future production cannot be stored up in financial assets that do not make the entire society any richer. Pensioners do not live from financial assets, but out of real production. This means that goods delivered to the pensioners have to be taken from profits or wages in the period when the goods are demanded and consumed. The government is not storing up goods when it runs a surplus. Quite the opposite one could argue, because a public surplus forced upon the private sector might cause unemployment and a smaller production.

The requirement of a *sustainable* budget might cause a double 'fallacy of composition', because a) it causes unemployment and lower economic growth in the actual period, without b) increasing the potential production in the future! This is the consequence of the Commission using microeconomic reasoning on a macroeconomic problem.

It is a grave misunderstanding of economic theory to argue that any society can increase its wealth by a surplus on the public sector budget that increases the governmental financial accumulation. These arguments sound more like old-fashioned mercantilist ideas, than modern economic thinking. Adam Smith has already demonstrated that financial assets do not make a country any wealthier. The 'Wealth of Nations' consists of *real assets* which can only be increased by real investments. The best policy to reduce the pressure of future commitments is to enlarge the real capital stock – it may be man-made, human capital or natural capital. The government cannot save through accumulation of financial assets, but through facilitating real capital accumulation in the private and the public sectors.

The above quote from the Commission leaves the reader unsettled with regard to the purpose of the required 'fiscal discipline', because there are no theoretically valid macroeconomic arguments to support the idea that fiscal discipline by itself should support economic growth. On the contrary, it seems pretty doubtful to what extent, if at all, the SGP increases macroeconomic stability. The *Financial Times* has taken the rather dramatic step, in an editorial comment, of calling it an 'Instability Pact'. According to conventional, Keynesian economics, SGP has, simply, turned the role of economic policy upside down. The purpose of the Pact is primarily to secure stability of the public budget *at the expense of the stability of macroeconomic development*.

One has to say that from a welfare point of view there are good reasons to call the rules of the SGP 'stupid', and the so-called *sustainable* budget argument does not change this conclusion when the impact on unemployment is taken into consideration.

Concluding remarks

The EMU does reduce the macroeconomic room for manoeuvre for the member countries to pursue an independent exchange rate and monetary policy. On top of that, the SGP limits the individual countries' possibility of conducting independent fiscal policies. Taken together these constraints severely reduce the macroeconomic policy with regard to growth and employment. The requirements of balance or even a surplus in the public sector budget is derived from a misplaced analogy between a *sound* household budget and public sector budget where the government takes responsibility for macroeconomic stability. The public sector will always be a mirror image of aggregate behaviour within the private sector. To limit the public sector deficit without any consideration of the imbalances between savings and investment in the private sector might cause increased unemployment and can hardly be justified as long as the country is in a recession.

If the EMU is to survive in a longer-term perspective the SGP probably have to be scrapped or at least relaxed quite a lot quite quickly.

Notes

1. *Financial Times*, 17 and 22 October 2002.
2. The performance of the macroeconomic development of the EMU countries has been a test case for the predictive power of different macroeconomic theories. It has long been a claim by (post)-Keynesian economists that unemployment would rise as a consequence of the restrictive policies within the EMU: see, for example, P. Arestis and M. Sawyer, 'The Deflationary Consequences of the Single Currency', in M. Baimbridge, B. Burkitt and P. Whyman, *European Monetary Integration*, Basingstoke: Macmillan,

2000; and J. Jespersen, *Introduktion til makroøkonomisk teori*, København: DJØFs Forlag, 2000. A contrasting claim, that the convergence process towards full employment among the participating countries would continue, was argued by neoclassical economists: see, for example, M.J. Artis and M. Buti, 'Setting Medium-Term Fiscal Targets in EMU', in A. Brunila, M. Buti and D. Franco (eds), *The Stability and Growth Pact – the Architecture of Fiscal Policy in EMU*, Basingstoke: Palgrave, 2001; and A. Brunila, M. Buti and J. Veld, 'Fiscal policy in Europe: how effective are automatic stabilizers?', *Economic Papers no. 177 – September*, Brussels: Directorate-General for Economic and Financial Affairs of the European Commission, 2002.

3. This is what, in the theoretical literature, is called the 'fallacy of composition', when microeconomic arguments are transferred uncritically to the macro-economics level. The best-known example is the 'paradox of thrift', where an increased propensity to save by individuals causes a fall in the national saving rate! See, J. Jespersen, 'Den atomistiske fejlslutning – en konsekvens af "den økonomiske fornuft" ', in C. Fenger-Grøn and J.E. Kristensen (eds), *Kritik af den økonomiske fornuft*, København: Hans Reitzels Forlag, 2001.

4. J.M. Keynes, *The General Theory of Employment, Interest and Money*, London: Macmillan, 1936, p. 249.

5. In the final chapter (24) of *The General Theory* Keynes mentions the possibility of 'socializing investments', which should not be misinterpreted. Keynes was a liberal, but when the private sector failed then he believed the state had to fill in the gap by undertaking the real investment which society needed, but the private sector was not able, through the market mechanism, to organize itself. Skidelsky sees Keynes as the late exponent in the great liberal tradition in British social thinking initiated by John Locke and continued by Malthus, Burke and Stuart Mill, where the state is a necessary institution even with a liberal society to secure the greatest individual freedom! R. Skidelsky, *John Maynard Keynes – the Economist as Saviour, 1920–37*, London: Macmillan, 1992.

6. N. Bartholdy and L. Falkenberg, 'Stabilitets-og vækstpagten status 2003', *Danmarks Nationalbank: Kvartalsoversigt*, 2, Kvartal, 2003. It has to be said that Danmarks Nationalbank (the central bank of Denmark) took a very active role in persuading the population of the beneficial effects of Denmark joining the EMU in the campaign leading up to the Danish referendum in 2000.

7. European Commission, *European Economy*, 3, Brussels: Directorate-General for Economic and Financial Affairs of the European Commission, 2002.

4
The Euro in its Fifth Year: Expectations Fulfilled?

Renate Ohr

Controversial expectations initially

In the run-up to the signing of the Maastricht Treaty, Germany experienced an ongoing discussion about chances and risks of a monetary union. A vast majority of economists expressed their criticism about the establishment of a single European currency, as stipulated in the Maastricht Treaty. The following brief survey of arguments in favour of and against monetary union in Europe is intended to summarize the discussion of the 1990s. It is very likely that these arguments will come up in one form or another in the Swedish debate as well.[1]

Advocates of monetary union in Europe put forward the following arguments:

- The unification of various currencies to a single currency area allows the reduction of frictional losses within the trading and international payment systems.
- As a consequence, the efficiency and benefits of the Single Market and the intra-EU-capital movements will increase.
- Due to a common currency, speculations on exchange rates are impossible within the currency area. Consequently, wrong decisions resulting from exchange rate speculations will become less likely.
- The euro will be 'as stable as the Deutschmark', as the European Central Bank has been tailored to the model of the German *Bundesbank*.

- Additionally, monetary policy has a supranational character within monetary union and is thus less affected by national conflicts of interest (especially when considering a trade-off between employment and price stability).
- It will be the countries with 'weak' currencies that will benefit especially from monetary union, for example, by lower levels of interest rates, without countries known for their 'strong' currencies being harmed.
- All in all, the process of integration throughout Europe will be fostered.

Whereas critics emphasize:

- The strength of a particular currency cannot simply be transferred to another currency.
- There is no evidence for a sustainable consensus on the importance of price stability throughout all EU countries.
- The different economic structures and varying economic cycles of participating economies pose different requirements for monetary and fiscal policies. A uniform monetary policy cannot meet the needs of all countries.
- Fiscal policy remains within the national domain. This potentially enables each country to undermine the stability-oriented monetary policy of the European Central Bank.
- There are no reliable mechanisms for imposing sanctions on those national authorities that put monetary stability at risk.
- The euro is not backed by 'Euroland', but rather by a union of sovereign countries with diverging interests on many important issues.
- This is the reason why permanently successful monetary and fiscal policies that meet the needs of all countries are not in sight. The diverging positions can endanger both the internal and the external stability of the euro.
- All in all, this does not support the process of European integration but, in fact, makes the case against it.

Now the interesting question is: in the fifth year of the European Monetary Union, can we judge whether the advocates or the critics had a more realistic view?

The evolution of the euro between 1999 and 2003

One major task of any central bank is to provide a smooth functioning of payment transactions within the currency area. Another task is to provide a currency guaranteeing both price stability and exchange rate stability. The European Monetary Union will especially be evaluated by the success (or failure) of the European Central Bank and thus by the degree of price and exchange rate stability in the euro area.

Price stability (that is, low inflation rate) and exchange rate stability (that is, no devaluation) are, at least in the long run, not independent from each other. A currency with a low inflation rate will always be an attractive currency for investments, thus stabilizing the exchange rate. As a rule of thumb, any currency with an internationally relatively high price stability has a tendency to appreciate in the medium and long term. This may well be different when there are no significant international differences in inflation rates. In this case, other factors will gain influence on the development of exchange rates, which are mainly based on the expectations of market participants about general economic development in the future.

The Deutschmark has long been the prototype of a hard and stable currency. It was especially characterized by high price stability and, therefore, also by a hard external value, at least in comparison to other European currencies. When compared to the yen and the US dollar, the Deutschmark showed significant temporary fluctuations in value, with appreciations being followed by periods of marked depreciation.

Since its introduction the euro shows a relatively high level of price stability, too. But currently this performance is not an exceptionally good performance. When compared internationally, the average rate of inflation of all industrial countries is not higher than the average rate of inflation within the euro currency area. This was frequently different with the Deutschmark, since it showed significantly lower inflation rates than other competing currencies. Additionally, the maximum rate of inflation of 2 per cent tolerated by the European Central Bank has been exceeded slightly in most cases. In spite of a tolerable inflation rate, which shows no sigus of any alarming developments the evidence of price stability is not yet fully credible and lasting.

On the other hand, one has to admit that the initial position of the European Central Bank was not easy: introducing a new currency that is to be credible right from the start and defining an efficient common monetary policy for a union of very different economies does comprise a lot of difficulties. For instance, it is not easy to convey continuity and credibility of monetary policy when it is obvious that the central bank has no assured knowledge about the transmission mechanism of monetary policy instruments within the currency area.[2]

There is another circumstance to consider with regard to the external stability of the euro: a continuous loss of value of the euro with a depreciation up to 30 per cent to the US dollar in the first three years of its existence. Loss of this magnitude had not even been expected by the critics of the European Monetary Union. In a system of flexible exchange rates both upward *and* downward fluctuations are very common phenomena (as mentioned before, the Deutschmark was affected by this, too). Still, there is a major difference: it is relevant whether it is a well-known currency that has earned a reputation throughout decades, both within a country and with investors throughout the world, that shows such a weakness or whether it is a new currency without such a record of success facing continuous depreciation right from its start and for a number of years.

Nevertheless, the unexpected and long-lasting starting weakness of the euro cannot be interpreted as a basic failure of this currency. Critical monitoring and a realistic assessment remains crucial, as the confidence crisis of the first three years was also caused by initially highly euphoric marketing of the euro which raised excessively positive expectations. Plus, the following appreciation of the euro when compared to the US dollar was based more on pessimistic attitudes of international investors towards dollar investments than on an increase of confidence concerning the euro.

Today, the external stability of a currency is to a large extent dependent on the confidence of investors. At times in which financial markets are largely moulded by expectations, the psychological acceptance of the common currency by market participants becomes a crucial factor for its long-run success. An enduring confidence in the currency does not only depend on the quality of the monetary policy but also on economic dynamics and prosperity as well as on political unity in the currency area.[3] After all, currency represents the economic power and stability of the corresponding economy. A lack of confidence in the ability of the responsible authorities to solve economic problems within the currency area is reflected by a lack of confidence in the currency itself. This especially applies to a young currency.

In addition to large structural and cyclical differences between the participating countries, which complicate a successful common monetary policy, further economic weaknesses can be observed within the euro area (for example, high levels of taxes and payroll deductions or a lack of flexibility on labour markets). This is less the case in other currency areas (such as the US dollar, pound sterling). Moreover, 'Euroland' as the corresponding economic area behind the euro has significant problems of identification with the new currency. All of these factors have contributed to a prolonged weakness of the euro. The United States is not free of problems either (this especially applies to its excessive current account deficits and an enormous increase of budget deficits), temporarily weakening confidence in the US dollar.

Challenges for the European Monetary Union

Even if the initial devaluation of the euro seems to be eliminated for the time being and the price stability within the European Monetary Union seems more or less to be guaranteed (though some participants of the monetary union temporarily showed inflation rates of above 4 per cent), both observations still do not provide evidence for the long-run stability of the single currency. The challenges for the monetary union are rather of a medium- or long-term character and are still to come.

These will emerge in three situations. The first test will appear when the business cycle shows recessive trends in large areas of the monetary union. Then the trade-off between employment aims on one hand and anti-inflation targets on the other hand will break up again.

Second, a global turnaround regarding the acceptance of inflation and expected rates of inflation with a general increase of inflationary trends will be another test for the euro.

The third test will be an excessively rapid extension of the 'Euro-club' with the inclusion of Eastern European EU accession countries. One cannot emphasize frequently enough that it is a very difficult task to define and to implement an efficient common monetary policy for an increasingly heterogeneous economic area. Provision of an adequate political foundation for monetary union will then be further deferred into the future.

It is only these scenarios that will reveal whether the monetary authorities will be able to follow a policy of a permanently consistent and successful track of price-level stability. The following section enlarges upon the first challenge mentioned above.

Threats to the Stability and Growth Pact

Evidence in support of the first challenge being a severe test for monetary union could be observed in 2003 when the Stability and Growth Pact[4] was initially to be applied to a large country. During the first two years of monetary union the proof of fiscal discipline had been supported by a generally good economic performance. Now, in a situation with decreasing growth rates, it is harder to keep to the fiscal targets. Current political efforts in Germany with regard to fiscal deficits over the 3 per cent limit for another fiscal year demonstrate that the sanctions of the Stability Pact are not taken seriously. Obviously it is very problematic if sanctions do not grip automatically, but rather have to be decided by the council of ministers. Potential sinners of tomorrow return a verdict on today's sinners.

But is compliance with the Stability and Growth Pact of such importance? The stability of a currency is always partly determined by the solidity of public spending. The longer an unsound fiscal policy lasts, the more likely is a loss of confidence in the economy as a whole. Then doubts arise whether the central bank is willing and able to follow a consequently stability-oriented monetary policy.

Within monetary union this problem gets even worse, as the single monetary policy is confronted with different national fiscal policies. For any single member country, there could be an advantage of free-riding, since within monetary union the community partly absorbs the crowding-out of increasing public debts, caused by interest and exchange rate effects.[5] Various previously segmented national capital markets, which have been separated by currency risks, unify to a common capital market within the new currency area. Thus, interest and exchange rate changes due to national indebtedness are less serious to the individual country increasing its debts, but the partner countries are now affected too. The possibility of shifting some of the negative consequences to partner countries may lead to a decrease of the costs of indebtedness of the single country and finally to an increase of the willingness to incur debts.[6] If such free-riding behaviour from single countries is not sanctioned, the effects of an unsound fiscal policy will be socialized within the monetary union, increasing the incentive to all member countries to increase their debts as well.

These considerations are often responded to with the counter-argument that, even within monetary union, for debt issues of unsound governments higher risks are taken into account. The interest rates for bonds will increase and consequently lower the incentive for debts. However, this is only true if the no-bail-out provision of the Maastricht Treaty is credible.[7] The credibility of this provision is controversial, since the European Union does explicitly regard itself as a joint community. But if the no-bail-out rule is not credible, countries with an excessive deficit will not face severe risks of insolvency and liquidity and will therefore not be confronted with an additional risk premium on bonds issued. The interest rate within the monetary union will then reflect the average indebtedness of the community.

Another reason for a potential decline of fiscal discipline within the European Monetary Union is a shift of responsibilities from the national level to the community level.[8] National governments are no longer compelled to be accountable for the negative consequences of their budget deficits on monetary stability, they can rather defer this responsibility to the European Central Bank, whereas in the case of national monetary policy and a national independent currency the quality of the currency is interpreted as an indicator for the quality of national government policies. Any government with its own currency is therefore under pressure to follow a stability-oriented policy, while in the case of monetary union this mechanism is not in effect.

This means that a sustained guarantee of fiscal discipline *within* the monetary union is of greater importance than the compliance to fiscal convergence criteria *before* entering the monetary union.[9] This sustained budgetary discipline was to be reached by the Stability and Growth Pact. The fact that initially Germany and by now further countries have problems adhering to the agreed budget lines has already lead to upcoming discussions on a softening of the Stability and Growth Pact. For instance, the general 3 per cent limit for budget deficits is claimed to be a too strict narrowing of the range of fiscal policies during phases of economic slowdown.

However, the member countries have committed themselves within the Stability and Growth Pact to have balanced budgets or even surpluses in the medium term. When starting from a roughly balanced position, there is, in general, no danger of exceeding the 3 per cent limit due to deficits caused by an economic slowdown. Problems only arise if a structural balance had not been reached before and an insufficient distance to the 3 per cent limit existed. This is the situation right now, as some member countries of the monetary union have refrained from reducing their budget deficits in a favourable economic situation during the first two years.

We will see whether this first test by a recession will lead to a softening of the Stability and Growth Pact. In this case confidence in the fiscal rules would be lost and the stability of the single currency would seriously be endangered.

Eastern enlargement of the EMU?

Another prevailing issue is the third challenge initially mentioned: the eastern enlargement will substantially alter the character of the European Union once again. The heterogeneity of the union will increase, economically weak countries will gain further weight within the union, other majorities and coalitions can dominate economically relevant decisions and new conflicts of interest may arise. This applies to the monetary union as well, if it is enlarged relatively quickly by the Eastern European accession countries.

The divergence of growth rates will increase and presumably the divergence of inflation rates, too. This may lead to contradictory ideas about the common monetary policy, exhibiting additional political pressure on the European Central Bank.[10]

The Eastern European accession countries are in the process of catching up economically and of structural changes. Major economic differences to the existing EU countries cannot simply be neglected. The growth rates are higher than in Western Europe, though the positive gap has lately decreased significantly.[11] Meanwhile, the inflation rate is in the single-digit range, but it is still clearly higher than in current EU countries. Unemployment rates are high and current accounts are (with the exception of Slovenia) in deficit. Not to be neglected are the still fragile structures of financial markets. All these aspects show that the requirements with regard to monetary policy of the Eastern Europe accession countries are not the same as those of today's members of the monetary union.

By fast entry into the European Monetary Union the Middle and Eastern European countries expect an increase of credibility concerning the stability of their economic policies. This would correspond with an explicit reduction of interest rates which would support economic development in general. These advantages were also realized by the former 'weak currency' countries in Western Europe which entered the monetary union. But they had the additional advantage of a euro depreciating in its initial phase, enhancing the competitiveness against other countries. The Eastern European accession countries may benefit from lower interest rates as well, but eventually with a relatively 'expensive' euro!

The expected net capital transfer into the new accession countries may become a risk too. What will happen, if the desired positive effects of entry into the monetary union do not occur quick enough or even do not occur at all? What will happen, if it becomes evident that taking over the euro is not sufficient if there is still a lack of good governance, if market imperfections are not eliminated and if investments do not achieve the returns expected?[12] Capital flows would turn back quickly and worsen the balance of payments. A depreciation or a national increase of interest rates will not be possible any more, putting the pressure of adjustments on the real economy of the accession countries.

It is frequently assumed that the accession countries are already embanked on a steady and quick process of catching up. Sometimes the discussion simply focuses on the exact number of years that are required for convergence with today's EU countries. However, this catching-up process is in no way a steady and quick one. When looking at per capita incomes of the Middle and Eastern European candidates in relation to the average per capita income of the current EU, a mixed picture can be seen. Leaving Bulgaria and Romania aside, the average per capita income of the remaining eight EU candidates ranges between 32 per cent (Latvia) and 71 per cent (Slovenia) of the average for the EU (figures for 2001). Furthermore, the convergence to the EU average does not follow a steady path. Convergence has initially increased after overcoming the shock of transformation but has temporarily decreased in some countries again over recent years.

Even if, at times, the Eastern European economies have shown impressive rates of growth, one should not make the mistake of predicting a similar positive economic development for the future. Quite the opposite: one has to assume that persisting, severe divergences of the real economies will prevail in the near future between current EU member countries (respectively the countries of the monetary union) on one hand and the Eastern European accession countries on the other hand. Thus, integration of the transformation countries into the monetary union, if it takes place too quickly, would take away a good part of the flexibility that these countries need for structural adjustments. Furthermore, the monetary union itself would be exposed to increased strain due to a greater heterogeneity of the member countries. Then the European Central Bank would have even more difficulties to define a monetary policy which is suitable for all countries involved. Consequently, one should not swamp the monetary union with this third challenge of eastern enlargement of the monetary union, without knowing whether the euro will survive the first two challenges mentioned above.

Future prospects

It is obvious already that the first challenge for the euro, the recession that can currently be observed in some countries of the monetary union, calls its stable foundations into question. Attacks on the Stability and Growth Pact, that is, attacks on the institutional framework that is to guarantee fiscal stability in the currency area, undermine the necessary credibility of the monetary union. Furthermore, the European single currency will remain weak, as long as it is not backed by a sound, united Euroland economy, a common political will and a European identity.

The enlargement of the monetary union to the east would magnify all risks that have been mentioned before the establishment of the union. This implies that, after the enlargement of the EU, the monetary union should remain a 'club in the club' and not immediately be further enlarged by the Eastern European countries. Otherwise the new currency will be overstrained. After all, the experiences of almost five years of European Monetary Union do not provide evidence for a solid and robust euro yet.

Notes

1. See, for example, P. Bofinger, St. Collignon and E.-M. Lipp (eds), *Währungsunion oder Währungschaos? Was kommt nach der D-Mark*, Wiesbaden, 1993: Gabler; and also, R. Caesar, and H.-E. Scharrer (eds), *Maastricht: Königsweg oder Irrweg zur Wirtschafts- und Währungsunion?*, Bonn: Europa Union Verlag, 1994.
2. R. Ohr, 'Monetäre Steuerungsprobleme in einer Europäischen Währungs-union', in Zohlnhöfer, W. (ed.), *Europa auf dem Wege zur Politischen Union? Schriften des Vereins für Socialpolitik*, 247, 1996, Berlin: Duncker & Humblot, pp. 75–87.
3. M. Feldstein, 'The European Central Bank and the Euro: The First Year', *Journal of Policy Modeling*, 22, 2000, pp. 345–54.
4. On the Stability and Growth Pact, see R. Ohr and A. Schmidt, 'Europäische Geld- und Währungspolitik', in R. Ohr and T. Theurl (eds), *Kompendium europäische Wirtschaftspolitik*, München: Franz Vahlen Verlag, 2001, pp. 428–30.
5. C. Wyplosz, 'Monetary Union and Fiscal Policy Discipline', in European Commission (ed.), *European Economy – Special edition, No.1, The Economics of EMU*, Brussels, 1991, pp. 165–85.
6. W. Horstmann and E. Schneider, 'Deficits and Free Riders: Fiscal Elements of a European Constitution', *Kyklos*, 47, 1994, pp. 355–67.
7. The no-bail-out provision (Article 103 in the Treaty on the European Union) prescribes that neither a member country, nor the community, should take on responsibility for the debts of another country.
8. R. Ohr, 'Zur Fiskaldisziplin in der Europäischen Währungsunion', in E. Kantzenbach (ed.), *Staatsüberschuldung, Veröffentlichung der Joachim Jungius-Gesellschaft der Wissenschaften*, 84, Hamburg: Vandenhoeck & Ruprecht, 1996, pp. 103–14.
9. P. De Grauwe, 'Monetary Union and Convergence Economics', *European Economic Review*, 40, 1996, pp. 1091–101.
10. B. Eichengreen and F. Ghironi, 'EMU and Enlargement', Paper prepared for a conference on Economic and Monetary Union, European Commission, Brussels, 21–2 March 2001.
11. Poland, the largest and most significant candidate country, stagnated recently. WIIW, 'Transition Countries in 2002: Losing Steam', *Wiener Institut für Internationale Wirtschaftsvergleiche. Research Report No. 285*, Wien, 2002.
12. M. Bolle and H.-D. Jacobsen, 'New Risks Ahead: The Eastward Enlargement of the Euro Zone', *Intereconomics*, 36, 2001, pp. 298–304.

5
The ECB and the Decline of European Democracy

James Forder

The costs and benefits of shared currencies were argued over in one way or another for many years before the creation of the European Monetary Union. Perhaps the most notable aspect of the debate was that theorizing never brought about a consensus on much more than what the questions are. No one ever seriously doubted that there are some very small gains to be had from saving currency exchange costs and related matters. On the other hand, the obvious danger was that the necessity of having the same monetary policy through-out the area would result in bad economic policy and bad economic outcomes – unemployment chief amongst them. The principal issue in the debate, then, was whether the accumulation of small gains would outweigh the possible large losses. The European Commission did its best to make the case that the dangers were small, essentially by arguing that economic policy does not have much effect on economic outcomes anyway.[1] And in the event most of the European Union adopted the euro without much further consideration.

As things have turned out, of course, it very quickly became obvious that the dangers are real and the costs severe. Almost as soon as the European Central Bank, which now sets interest rates for the whole eurozone, started running policy, it found its position was impossible – some economies were booming, calling for higher interest rates, others heading towards recession, calling for lower ones. But the ECB could only set one rate. The result is that policy, however skilful and well-intentioned the policymakers happen to be, is inferior to what could be achieved with separate currencies.

As to the optimistic view that policy had little effect, and so it would not matter that the interest rate was inappropriate, nothing has happened to bear this out. The German case is particularly striking. There, had there been no monetary union and German policy had been set according to the needs of the German economy, there is simply no doubt that interest rates would have been lower than they have been. Had the interest rate been lower, growth would have been faster, unemployment would have been lower, the government deficit would have been lower, and the fears that prices might start falling, bringing Germany into the same deflationary predicament that has blighted Japan for a decade, would have remained very much further away. Of course, these costs, even in their bare economic measurement – to say nothing of the human costs of unemployment – dwarf the tiny gains that EMU is said to bring. Sadly, the German case, although the most important in virtue of Germany's size, is far from exceptional: perhaps also because the ECB allowed the interest rate to remain too high in the euro area as a whole, slow growth and high unemployment have been all too common in the eurozone.

So much for the theoretical debate over monetary union: decades of rational argument failed to satisfy some that it was too dangerous, and now the price for this symbol is being paid in unemployment. Those countries – Sweden, Denmark and the United Kingdom, along with the new EU members in Central and Eastern Europe – that were fortunate enough not to be swept into EMU in 1999 at least now have the chance of seeing the dangers clearly and avoiding the same fate.

But if the economic case against a single currency is now depressingly clear, there are further, perhaps even more important arguments that relate to the particular form of monetary union that has been adopted in the European Union. Some of them are matters of economic policy. For example, the eurozone chose to inflict he Stability and Growth Pact (SGP) on itself. This tragically misnamed agreement sought to prevent governments from borrowing more than small amounts even in recessions. The main effect is to prevent a proper budgetary response to those recessions. The President of the European Commission has himself, quite rightly, called the Pact 'stupid',[2] and it certainly aggravated what was already a bad situation in some countries. As it happens, the Pact seems likely to collapse altogether since France and Germany decided in November 2003 to ignore the obligations it put on them. Whether it continues to exert any influence on policymaking remains to be seen, but it has certainly done nothing for the cordiality of relations between the European partners. And, purely from the point of view of economic policy, it would certainly have been better if it had never been conceived.

As if to make the whole position worse, the European Central Bank is given by the Maastricht Treaty the overriding objective of achieving 'price stability'.[3] This expression was not further defined in the Treaty, but the ECB simply announced that it had the right to determine what it means, and it meant inflation of 'below 2%'.[4] More recently, presumably fearing deflation, the ECB has very slightly changed its tune, and now says its target is to have inflation below, but 'close to' 2 per cent.[5] One concern is clearly that since the ECB has its objective stated purely in terms of inflation, it can be expected to be much more averse to risks of price increases than to risks of unemployment. And the European Central Bank has made it clear in statement after statement that it considers the control of inflation absolutely paramount and that it will not pursue other objectives. This has made it the subject of a chorus of academic, political and business criticism.[6] It should be no surprise, consequently, if business confidence in the euro area remains low. Why should anyone undertake a risky investment when the policymaker has, in effect, committed itself to raising interest rates when there is the mere suspicion of inflation?

Other considerations are of a more political nature, and one in particular that has received far less attention than it should concerns the constitution and operation of the European Central Bank. The arrangements made for the operation of monetary policy stand in the sharpest contrast to the principles of democracy to which the European Union claims to adhere, and are not only a breach of principle, but also threaten to undermine effective policy, and indeed the European Union itself.

The words of the Treaty itself tell the story in astonishing language. Referring to the 'European System of Central Banks', which is the collection of national central banks and the ECB, Article 108 of the Treaty makes their status perfectly plain. It says:

> When exercising the powers and carrying out the tasks and duties conferred upon them by this Treaty and the Statute of the ESCB, neither the ECB, nor a national central bank, nor any member of their decision-making bodies shall seek or take instructions from

Community institutions or bodies, from any government of a
Member State or from any other body. The Community institutions
and bodies and the governments of the Member States undertake
to respect this principle and not to seek to influence the members
of the decision-making bodies of the ECB or of the national central
banks in the performance of their tasks.[7]

It is perfectly true, of course, that extensive arguments have been made
to the effect that central bank independence is desirable, and the idea
happened to become popular among economists and policymakers
just as the design of EMU was being considered. But these arguments
were never as convincing as some pretended, even on their own
terms. And perhaps more importantly they entirely failed to respond
to some crucial issues.

The basic argument for independence was that policymaking
removed from political control would be better policymaking – and
in particular it would be less inflationary. This was supposed to
follow from the idea of the 'political business cycle' – the idea that
low interest rates help win elections, but only by doing lasting
economic damage. Plausible as many found this idea, it was only
ever supported by a small number of anecdotes, and no convincing
evidence for it was ever presented.[8]

Even if the data existed to make this case for independence, however,
it would hardly complete the argument. On the contrary, it would
leave important questions unanswered. One is this: supposing it were
shown that elections are won by poor policy, why should this be
limited to monetary policy? Why would this not lead to a general
argument against democracy? Similarly, another version of the case
for independence simply says that experts run policy better than
amateurs. Even supposing that democracy means amateurs never
take expert advice, the same question would again arise: why would
this be an argument specifically about monetary policy?

One response to these points is to agree. And, indeed, perfectly
sincere arguments against democracy have frequently been made
along these lines. The first of them is to be found in Plato's *Republic*,
and since then such arguments have never been far away in discussions
of the theory of democracy.

On the other hand, there would be difficulties with this response
as well. The first is perhaps no more than an inconvenience. It is

that nowhere have the creators of the ECB, the recent promoters of European integration, or even the staff of the ECB themselves, given any indication that the design of the ECB grows out of an attitude of general hostility to democracy. The European Union presents itself as committed to democratic values, and if that is the case, the design of the ECB clearly cannot be defended on the opposite basis.

Next, if one were going to pursue such a line of thinking, it would be necessary to consider all the arguments. The idea that the case for democracy is based exclusively on the presumption that it promotes good policy would be thought deeply eccentric by the vast majority of democratic theorists. They have said that participation in government is valuable in itself, that a democratic constitution gives substance to the principle of equality of individuals, and even that it helps to legitimize decisions that are harmful to some. Any of these, and indeed, one might have hoped, all of them, would be valued and welcomed in the European Union. But as regards monetary union, at least, this is not what has happened. Nor would it be right to say that these things have been ignored in the design. Rather, as Article 108 makes distressingly clear, they have been specifically, deliberately and abruptly excluded.

Even this, however, is far from the end of the issue. Another crucial consideration is that whatever the limitations of democracy may be, it takes an immense credulity to believe that 'experts' who are specifically protected from suffering the consequences of their errors (or indeed their misfeasance) are truly the policymakers who have the best incentives to protect and advance the public interest. The inestimable strength of the democratic system is not that the popular will is effortlessly enacted into policy, but simply that when those who govern us turn out to be bad at their jobs, we can fire them. But again, this central and essential popular power has, as regards monetary policymaking in the eurozone, been terminated. There, however poor the policy, the policymakers keep their jobs. In this context, that is what it is meant by 'independence', and one can see why central bankers themselves are so much in favour of it.

It is true that the ECB does make much of the fact that it is 'accountable' as well as independent. 'Accountability and independence are two sides of the same coin', as its says.[9] Furthermore, it routinely insists that it meets the highest standards of accountability – in this regard, 'the Eurosystem meets or exceeds the best practices of any central bank' as it said in one of its earliest statements.[10] That is all very well as far as it goes, but closer inspection reveals a severe deficiency. That is that what the ECB means by 'accountable' is that it makes statements about what it does and answers some of the questions put to it. All is revealed by its definition of 'accountability'. It says, it is an obligation to 'justify and explain' its decisions to citizens and their elected representatives.[11] Nothing at all is said about the consequences of bad decisions. Nothing is even said about the assessment of the justifications and the explanations.[12]

A good, although, taking a balanced view, it must be said, only a minor, instance relates to the ECB's price stability target. Its Annual Report of 1998 – before the euro was even introduced – said that its target would be to keep inflation below 2 per cent and this 'quantitative definition' of price stability 'gives the public a measure for assessing the success of the single monetary policy, thereby strengthening the accountability of the Eurosystem'.[13] Beside this statement of how it is to be held accountable, one can put the outcome: inflation as measured by the ECB was above 2 per cent in 2000, 2001, 2002 and in the first ten months of 2003.[14] It was, it is true, within target in 1999, but, owing to the time-lags between policy and effect, that is attributable to the policy settings before the ECB was in control. After that, it has missed its target every year.

Of course, the ECB would defend itself by saying that it is not in precise control of inflation and it can only be expected to meet its target in the 'medium term'.[15] It is no doubt obvious that this has the effect of obscuring any accountability that might have been available from the 'quantitative target', but in any case, how long is the 'medium term'? Interestingly enough, at a very early stage in the life of the ECB, Vice President Noyer did give an indication of what is meant by 'medium term'. Addressing the Committee on Economics and Monetary Affairs of the European Parliament in September 1999, he made what must now be one of the most regretted statements of an ECB official:

> it is entirely possible that you would slightly exceed the lower limit or the upper limit of 2%, let's say for one month or two, because we won't be able to react in such a term, but if you see that it has gone above the 2% mark just for a month or two and then it drops back down again and it remains within an acceptable

range after that, that's what I meant by saying that we have a medium-term price stability policy.[16]

So getting on for four years would be much longer than is required for an assessment of the 'medium term' success.

Now, the misses have been small, and it is not my view that it is proper to give so much emphasis to inflation control as the ECB says it does in any case. But the point is that my view is not the ECB's view – they think inflation control is essential, and indeed their overriding objective. And, more importantly still, the ECB's own description of their all important 'accountability', meagre as it is, rests on meeting this target. And they have consistently failed. And yet nothing happens. What is the use of that kind of 'accountability'?

It might be said, of course, that no discussion of accountability is complete unless consideration is also given to the possibility of a Treaty reform, removing the powers of the central bank. If the rules can be changed, it might be argued, there is no real problem. There is some truth in that, although it should be remembered that the possibility of restoring accountability or democratic legitimacy does not mean that it has never been destroyed. Democracy always might be restored, but that certainly does not mean that it is never compromised. In any case, the position of the European Central Bank is rather unusual in this regard as well. Some independent central banks, such as the Bank of England, are in a position where the legislation has specifically reserved the right of the government to overrule the Bank. The motive for this is that the independence of the Bank then reflects the general predominance of a stable price policy and protects the long-term orientation of policy. But the possibility of an overrule preserves the democratic credentials of the arrangement and the incentives of the bankers. The case of the ECB is, of course, right at the other extreme. Unless there is to be a Treaty amendment, its independence is absolute.

At first sight, it might seem that the independence of the ECB is therefore completely secure. A Treaty amendment would require unanimity of the member states, and referendums in some of them before there could be ratification. And it is often presumed that this is inconceivable. If this were the whole truth, it would be bad enough, since it would emphasize the problem of accountability even more. Not only would the ECB be free, by its statutes, from any meaningful obligation of democracy, but also free of any sanction for poor policy.

And indeed, that may be the truth, but I suggest that there is, in fact, a further problem in that the ECB does not feel its independence is secure, and is thereby motivated to act so as to protect it.

The difficulty for the ECB arises because the extreme form which independence takes gives its undeniably powerful position a paradoxical aspect. Certainly, it has a high degree of independence, indeed a remarkable degree. But this remarkable position is also obviously offensive to democratic values. If nothing else, the wording of Article 108 makes this apparent, and that creates a permanent political motive for reform.

Indeed, Willem Buiter, a former member of the Bank of England's monetary policy committee, specifically drew attention to the danger to the ECB's position saying that its failure to make itself sufficiently accountable could 'pose a threat to its continued operational independence'.[17] The ECB was not receptive to his particular suggestions, but that is not mean to say that it does not understand the danger to which he drew attention. Perhaps more directly threatening was the remark made by Valéry Giscard d'Estaing, contemplating the beginning of the Constitutional Convention. Thinking of the priority given to the objective of price stability, he told *Le Figaro* that 'It seems to me that we have not yet clarified the role of the ECB...Having a priority does not mean that it should abstain from all other objectives.'[18] It is an unfortunate fact that nothing seems to have been done about this issue in the draft constitution, but again, it can be presumed that the ECB understands that its position is not impregnable.

Concern for its own survival, or survival in the current, excessively powerful form, I suggest, goes a long way towards explaining the quantity of effort the ECB puts into advocating its basically vacuous notion of accountability. On the face of it, if its independence were secure, it could simply get on with the job. Yet it constantly reiterates the view that it is 'accountable', even though, to say the least, it has no expertise at all in political philosophy.[19] And the idea it is so keen to advance never reaches beyond a duty to 'justify and explain'. It never reaches to the possibility of there being a sanction either for policy failure or for a poor justification or an inadequate explanation.[20] One possibility is that the ECB has simply not contemplated the possibility of itself taking a bad decision. Or perhaps it is merely that it is not prepared to consider the possibility that anyone else should ever be in a position to assess them. But surely a better explanation is that it is trying to use its status, prestige and authority to distort understanding of what should be required of it. And it is doing this to protect its own position.

Indeed, similar points can be made about other policy areas where threats to the ECB's position might arise. One is how to handle the representation of the new member states on the ECB's board, another from the much better examples of independent central banking on offer in Europe in the form of the Bank of England and the Bank of Sweden, and a third from the difficulties of maintaining the Stability and Growth Pact.

The difficulty over the growth in the size of the EU arises from the fact that in its original design, the policymaking board of the ECB consists of six 'executive' members, and 12 others – one from each participating country. A board of 18 is already probably too large, but if further members were to be added from each new participant from Central and Eastern Europe, it would certainly become unwieldy. The solution to this that has been agreed is that if the eurozone grows much further, voting rights will rotate between members. Since different countries will hold voting rights with different frequencies, and broadly speaking the smaller countries will have them less often,[21] the difficulty is that in an unrepresented country, a further question as to the legitimacy of the ECB's policy may arise. And once the right questions are asked, it will be impossible for the ECB to continue to peddle its self-serving discussions of 'accountability'. After all, once attention is directed to the issue, it is not hard to see that a country is not democratic because its people are allowed to ask a question about a policy: it is only democratic when they can change it. The new voting rules, however, only apply if the eurozone expands, and it is reasonable, therefore, to anticipate that the ECB would like to resist such expansion.

The cases of Britain, Sweden and Denmark are slightly different. First, the new voting rules would not require any rotation as a result of only three new countries joining. Second, these central banks, and particularly the Bank of England, have run more successful policy, and done it with an open attitude and approach, which is widely contrasted with the poor policy and grudging disclosures of the ECB.[22] This has also brought a general approval of the financial markets for the way in which policy has been conducted. There are, therefore, examples of how the ECB could be reformed. And indeed, in an attack that no doubt stung the ECB badly, EU Trade Commissioner Pascal Lamy and Jean Pisani-Ferry, specifically called for reform '*à la Britannique*'.[23] It is obvious that the ECB's position would be safer if these examples could be eliminated, and one should expect them, therefore, in contrast to their likely attitude to Central and Eastern Europeans, to welcome British membership of the euro.

The formal position with the Stability and Growth Pact is this. It places limits on the amount that governments can borrow. Not only are the targets sometimes unachievable, because the limits are too narrow, but seeking to achieve them is damaging – when a recession begins, tax revenues naturally fall, this pushes the government budget towards deficit and, unless it begins from an unusually favourable position, this creates a danger of breaching the Pact limits. This then means that the government must undertake expenditure cuts or tax increases. And either of those have a tendency to make the recession worse – just the opposite of what is required. Numerous suggestions for reform have been made, ranging from scrapping it altogether to changing the rules so that the limits reflect the position of the business cycle. None of these were agreed, while only the smaller countries seemed to be directly the victims of the arrangement. But in November 2003, with France and Germany both in breach of the rules, its operation was effectively suspended.

The difficulty for the ECB is that if the Pact is abandoned, as it now seems to have been, or even reformed, the scope for conflict between it and the member state governments will be substantially increased. There are a number of aspects to this problem. One is simply that the failure of the SGP instantiates the passing of the intellectual consensus that created the ECB. But another is that the SGP had the effect of paralyzing fiscal policy. The deficits that it allowed were small, and while governments were trying to meet their obligations, they have been engaged in a constant battle to lower spending. The result is that there has been no direct conflict of objectives between the ECB and the governments. Should the SGP cease to act on the minds of the governments, they will surely rediscover the desirability of using, or at least trying to use, fiscal policy to lower unemployment. Then, to the extent that the ECB sticks to its goal of controlling inflation, it will inevitably find itself in conflict with the member state governments. And that will create a further threat to its independence.

One must anticipate, then, that the ECB will continue to defend what remains of the SGP to the best of its ability. Indeed, in its *Monthly Bulletin* of June 2003, it was doing so at some length.[24] Although it had already, by then, been forced by the actions of the German government to accept that the Pact terms would be breached, it nevertheless called for 'strict implementation', saying it is 'indispensable', and it called for a return to the budgetary limits by 2004.[25]

One aspect of this is that it is really nothing to do with the ECB. Its role is to set monetary policy. The Treaty prohibits attempts to 'influence' it. But the ECB does not draw any inference that it should leave other policy areas to the proper authorities there. Rather, it uses the position of power and prestige it is given to push its view in these areas.[26] Perhaps a more important point, however, is that the ECB has every incentive to distort proper policy discussion. It is perfectly clear that its 'explain and justify' story is a misrepresentation of the conventional understanding of accountability. Although that may not in itself damage policy (as distinct from legitimacy), a similar misrepresentation over fiscal policy is likely to do just that. Here, the ECB at least gives the impression of expertise, and its arguments can be expected to carry some weight. But it has an incentive to defend the SGP which has nothing to do with the merits of that system, but rather, everything to do with the ECB's defence of its power.

A particular aspect of the ECB's attitude to fiscal policy is its attitude to the welfare state. In its *Monthly Bulletin* of April 2003 it gave close attention to the future of these arrangements and it is probably no surprise that its conclusion was that drastic reforms are required, and required quickly, which will 'limit the public sector's exposure', as they put it.[27] As to the thought that the issues involved might be political ones and, if nothing else, involve value judgements about the appropriate balance between private and public financing, the ECB promptly dismisses public financing as 'harmful to economic growth' and then says that because the reforms are 'likely to face opposition from some groups in society' there is a 'risk' that it will take a long time to achieve them.[28] There is no hint, then, that there might be genuine differences of view, and the democratic process is simply treated as a problem, creating a 'risk', rather than the mechanism by which decisions are properly taken.

Now, any of these things – the expansion of the euro, the reform of the SGP and the future of welfare states, among many others – are proper matters for debate. Perhaps small countries should be less frequently represented in policymaking; perhaps the SGP is the basis of sound policy, and not 'stupid' at all; and perhaps the welfare state has outlived its day. Some people will, of course, agree with the ECB's conclusions. That is really not the issue. No doubt it will also be said that the ECB does have certain expertise, and it is reasonable for its view to be heard. That is a rather more doubtful point. The ECB is established as an agent to implement certain policy. If, for some reason, its view is wanted on other policy, it could be specifically asked for.

But the important issues revolve around the nature of the democratic process and how the creation of the ECB has disfigured it in the euro-zone. The construction of the ECB is offensive in itself and shameful to the whole European Union. Its own defence of its 'accountability' is quite clearly self-serving and valueless. But that defence is also an indicator that the ECB is a long way short of feeling secure in its position, and yet, is committed to its defence. And that clue is, then, first of all a warning that the ECB's views on other points are unlikely to be as objective as it would like us to believe. But second, it is much more than that. It is also a further critique of the construction of the ECB, since it is that construction that has put the ECB in the position of having a great deal of power and therefore of having power to defend its position. As Mancur Olson noted, once sectional interests become sufficiently well organized to seek to advance their own position, there is, 'for practical purposes, no limit to the harm they might do society'.[29] He was thinking of economic harm, but damage to the political fabric of democracy might be included as well.

So, should the euro area be expanded further? As far as expansion to Sweden and Britain is concerned, the ECB would surely welcome it. In complete contrast to the view expressed by supporters of the euro in these two countries, that membership will increase 'influence', the best way for these countries to influence the euro area is to continue to set better policy in a more legitimate framework. The ECB cannot be expected to welcome that continuation, but the people of Europe should.

But 'influence' is in any case far from being the issue. If it could be achieved by membership, would it be appropriate to pay for it with unemployment? Hardly. Those who imagine they will have personal influence from membership will just have to accept their current lot. In any case, the economics of the eurozone have greatly disappointed its advocates and, it should be said, they have disappointed its opponents too, notwithstanding that their warnings were confirmed. For more countries to venture into the euro after this confirmation would clearly be foolish. But not even the poor economic performance that the euro brings is the whole issue. There is a much wider issue as to the role of the institutions of the state and of citizens in democratic governance. Whether the construction of the ECB was the outcome of temporary insanity, or of a true conviction that central bankers can do no wrong and should be privileged above all others in government, or whether it was simply too much influenced by the central bankers who were part of the process,[30] a terrible disservice to the people of Europe has been done. One must hope that the calls for reform are ultimately successful. But until they are, for more countries with old and well-established democracies, or for that matter, those with new ones, to give up their own arrangements would be tragic.

Notes

1. See, for example, their assessment of the economics of EMU: M. Emerson, D. Gros, J. Pisani-Ferry and H. Reichenback, *One Market, One Money*, Oxford: Oxford University Press, 1992, especially chapter 6.
2. As President Prodi described it in *Le Monde* on 18 October 2002, www.lemonde.fr/recherche_articleweb/1,9687,294763,00.html
3. Article 105.
4. A decision of 13 October 1998, reported, for example, in the ECB *Monthly Bulletin*, January 1999, p. 38.
5. ECB, *Monthly Bulletin*, May 2003, p. 5.
6. A sample of which can be found at http://www.no-euro.com/factsfigures/quotes/ecb.asp
7. It was Article 107 in the Maastricht Treaty, but renumbered at Amsterdam.
8. A comprehensive test of it, which rejected the hypothesis, was undertaken by A. Alesina, G. Cohen and N. Roubini, 'Evidence on political business and monetary cycles', in A. Cukierman, Z. Heskovitz and L. Leiderman (eds), *Political Economy, Growth and Business Cycles*, Cambridge, MA: MIT Press, 1992.
9. ECB, *Monthly Bulletin*, November 2002, p. 46.
10. For example, in its *Monthly Bulletin* of January 1999, p. 42.
11. ECB, *Monthly Bulletin*, November 2002, p. 45. There are many similar statements – all to the same effect that telling people what it is doing is the essence of being 'accountable' to them.

12. And as to reaching the highest standards, even on these limited terms, it is a sad truth that the comment of *Le Monde* on 4 February 2002 expresses much the most common sentiment: 'When Alan Greenspan talks about economic recovery, the shareholders rise up and immediately buy dollars. When Mr Duisenberg says that he is confident about a rebound in the eurozone economy, the same dealers laugh.'

13. ECB, *Annual Report*, 1998, p. 49.

14. ECB, *Monthly Bulletin*, November 2003, p. 25.

15. Along with the assertions of the importance of accountability and the 'quantitative target', this is a routine move in the ECB's discussions of its 'accountability'. For example, ECB, *Monthly Bulletin*, June 2003, p. 46.

16. The remarks are available at the European Parliament web site: http://www.europarl.eu.int/comparl/econ/emu/noyer/default_en.htm

17. W. Buiter, 'Alice in Euroland', *Journal of Common Market Studies*, issue 1, 37, 1999, p. 205.

18. *Le Figaro*, 8 January 2002.

19. In addition to the claims quoted above, there are many other similar claims in the *Monthly Bulletins*; ECB chief economist Otmar Issing wrote an article, arguing, absurdly, that the ECB aims to be 'among the most transparent and accountable central banks in the world'. See, 'The Eurosystem: transparent and accountable or "Willem in Euroland"?', *Journal of Common Market Studies*, issue 4, 37, 1999, pp. 503–19. Much of the same issue is treated in O. Issing, V. Gaspar, I. Angeloni and O. Tristani, *Monetary Policy in the Euro Area*, Cambridge: Cambridge University Press, 2001. None of these give any indication of appreciating that 'explaining', 'justifying' and 'answering questions' come nowhere near establishing democratic credentials – they simply reassert the view that serves the ECB's interest.

20. I have more to say about the inadequacy of the ECB's 'explanations' as well as the defects in its idea of 'accountability' in J. Forder, 'Interests and "Independence": the European Central Bank and the theory of bureaucracy', *International Review of Applied Economics*, 16, 2002, pp. 51–69.

21. The details are rather complicated, but set out in the ECB, *Monthly Bulletin*, June 2003.

22. See, for example, the study of this by S. Eijffinger and J. de Haan, 'The democratic accountability of the European Central Bank: A comment on two fairy-tales', *Journal of Common Market Studies*, issue 3, 38, 2000, pp. 393–407. Buiter, 'Alice in Euroland', comments at length on the superiority of the Bank of England arrangements for accountability and transparency.

23. Reported in *The Guardian*, 24 January 2002.

24. Again, there are many statements to the same effect in earlier *Bulletins*.

25. ECB, *Monthly Bulletin*, June 2003, pp. 60 and 58.

26. Very much the same view could be said of its recurring forays into the advocacy of labour market deregulation.

27. ECB, *Monthly Bulletin*, April 2003, p. 39.

28. *Ibid.*, p. 41.
29. M. Olson, *The Logic of Collective Action*, Cambridge, Mass.: Harvard University Press, 1965, p. 44.
30. The Delors Committee, which drew up a plan not much different from the one implemented, was dominated by central bankers.

6

A Critical Analysis of EMU and of Sweden Joining It

Roland Vaubel

Sweden is not well suited to be a member of the European Monetary Union (EMU) because the relative price between Swedish goods and eurozone goods requires large adjustments. No current member of the eurozone faces a larger adjustment need than Sweden. Apparently, the Swedish pattern of production differs considerably from that of the eurozone. Swedish goods tend to become cheaper relative to eurozone goods on a long-term basis. Thus, if Sweden joins the euro-zone, Sweden will suffer from deflation when the rest of the eurozone enjoys price-level stability.

Moreover, if relative prices have to adjust a great deal, the same is true for relative wages. If Sweden joins the eurozone, it cannot any longer lower its relative wages by devaluing the krona. If Swedish nominal wages do not become much more flexible, Sweden will suffer from higher unemployment.

This has to be explained in some more detail. The economic costs and benefits of joining another currency area are the subject of the theory of optimum currency areas. I have argued elsewhere[1] that there are essentially two criteria to be applied: the cost of joining is accounted for by the need for relative price adjustment *vis-à-vis* the currency area to be entered, while the benefits depend on the openness of the economy (*vis-à-vis* the foreign currency area). All the other criteria that have been mentioned in the literature are important only because, and to the extent to which, they affect these two fundamental criteria.

Openness is a comprehensive indicator of the benefits because it affects the costs of information, transactions, exchange rate risk and convertibility risk which can be eliminated by joining another currency area. If openness is measured by the average of exports to, and imports from, the eurozone relative to GDP, Sweden takes a middle position in Europe.[2] The Swedish figure (14 per cent) is, for example, larger than the Greek (9 per cent), the British (10 per cent) or the Spanish figure (12 per cent) but it is much smaller than the Belgian (37 per cent), the Slovenian (30 per cent), the Hungarian (27 per cent) or the Czech (24 per cent).

Why is the need for relative price adjustment a comprehensive indicator of the cost of joining? If a country like Sweden joins a foreign currency area like the eurozone, it loses the exchange rate instrument. Its (nominal) exchange rate *vis-à-vis* the eurozone is immutably fixed. However, the exchange rate instrument is important to the extent to which Sweden and the eurozone produce different goods and experience different changes in the demand for, and supply of, these goods. If the exchange rate between the Swedish kroner and the euro cannot be adjusted any longer, the required and inevitable adjustment of relative prices must take the form of differential price level changes, that is, differences in inflation rates. Thus, in a common currency area, Sweden and the eurozone could not both enjoy price-level stability or attain the same target inflation rate.

Moreover, if, say, the world demand for goods shifts between Swedish and eurozone goods, not only relative prices but also relative wages have to be adjusted. If this cannot be achieved by way of (nominal) exchange rate adjustment, nominal wages have to carry the burden of adjustment. If Swedish nominal wages do not adjust flexibly to a loss of world demand, the loss of the exchange rate instrument leads to higher unemployment.

Table 6.1 shows the trend of relative prices between the Swedish and the French basket of goods (CPI). I have chosen the French basket of goods as a reference because France occupies the median position, in terms of both past inflation and revealed inflation aversion, in the Governing Council of the European Central Bank.[3] But it does not matter which basket or numeraire we chose as a reference as long as it is the same for all comparisons. Table 6.1 reveals that, in 1973–98, the price of Swedish goods has fallen relative to French goods at an annual rate of 1.0 per cent per annum. As can also be seen, this is the largest absolute relative price change *vis-à-vis* France for any EU member state except the UK and Ireland. But while Sweden's relative

Table 6.1 Relative price changes
vis-à-vis France, all EU member
states, 1975–98, per cent per annum

United Kingdom	+1.6
Ireland	+1.0
Italy	+0.7
Spain	+0.6
Greece	+0.6
Austria	+0.6
Denmark	+0.4
Portugal	+0.3
Germany	+0.1
France	0
Netherlands	−0.2
Belgium	−0.3
Luxembourg	−0.5
Finland	−0.6
Sweden	−1.0

Source: Vaubel, 'The Future of the Euro'.

prices decline *vis-à-vis* (the median of) the eurozone, the UK (+1.6 per cent) and Ireland (+1.0 per cent) tend to experience an increase. Thus, if the French median in the ECB Council keeps the French price level stable in terms of the euro, the UK and Ireland face inflation but Sweden – worse still – will suffer from deflation. In 2001 and 2002, the French inflation rate has been 1.8 and 1.9 per cent, respectively.

Table 6.2, which is taken from a paper by Viktor Winschel, includes also some of the new EU entrants and Turkey but confines the analysis of relative prices to the period 1992–8.[4] All annual rates of relative price change are measured *vis-à-vis* the US dollar as a common numeraire. Once more, Sweden is near the lower fringe – this time together with Spain. In absolute terms, Sweden's relative price change *vis-à-vis* France (1.53 per cent) is even larger than the relative price change between France and non-EU states like Turkey (0.31), Malta (0.73) and Cyprus (1.35). In other words, over this shorter but more recent period, the economic cost of joining the eurozone would have been smaller for Turkey, Malta and Cyprus than for Sweden. It would also have been smaller for Denmark (0.51) but not for the UK (2.39).

Table 6.2   Relative price changes *vis-à-vis* the US dollar, 1992–8, per cent per annum

Spain	−1.21
Sweden	−0.99
Italy	−0.30
Finland	+0.39
Portugal	+0.40
France	+0.52
Ireland	+0.53
Luxembourg	+0.54
Belgium	+0.58
Germany	+0.72
Austria	+0.82
Turkey	+0.83
Netherlands	+0.85
Denmark	+1.03
Malta	+1.25
Cyprus	+1.88
Hungary	+2.35
Greece	+2.40
United Kingdom	+2.92

Source: Winschel, 'EMU Enlargement', table 1.

In Table 6.3, Winschel applies a method of determining optimum currency areas that I suggested and used in my 1978 article (*op. cit.*). Starting with the core of three countries that experienced the smallest relative price adjustments among themselves, the group is successively enlarged by one country after another so as to minimize the increase in relative price adjustment within the group. In other words, we always add the country which minimizes the standard deviation of relative price changes *vis-à-vis* a common numeraire over all members of a group of this size.

The results are reported in Table 6.3. It reveals that Sweden would be the 17th country to be included in the monetary union – before Spain and the UK but after Turkey, Malta, Cyprus and Hungary. Spain is the only eurozone member that is less suitable than Sweden. Thus, both long-run trends and more recent data leave no doubt that the cost of joining the eurozone would be relatively high for Sweden. From an economic point of view, it is not a coincidence that Sweden did not become a member of the eurozone in 1999.

Table 6.3   Minimizing the standard deviation of relative price changes *vis-à-vis* the US, 1992–8, per annum

Standard deviation	Countries
0.01	France, Luxembourg, Ireland
0.01	+Belgium
0.02	+Portugal
0.07	+Finland
0.08	+Germany
0.11	+Austria
0.13	+Turkey
0.15	+Netherlands
0.17	+Denmark
0.20	+Malta
0.26	+Italy
0.37	+Cyprus
0.49	+Hungary
0.63	+Greece
0.73	+Sweden
0.84	+Spain
0.95	+United Kingdom

Source: Winschel, 'EMU Enlargement', table 4.

The need for relative price adjustment has already been a serious problem for the current members of the eurozone. In 2002, inflation was 1.6 per cent in Belgium and Germany but 4.7 per cent in Ireland. In 2001, consumer prices rose 1.8 per cent in France but 5.1 per cent in the Netherlands. These countries would have needed different monetary policies but in a monetary union this was impossible.

What about average inflation in the eurozone? The low inflation in 1999–2000 (1.75 per cent per annum on average) was simply inherited from the German *Bundesbank*. After all, the price level reacts to monetary policy with a lag of about two years. However, the European Central Bank is responsible for the inflation of 2001 and 2002, which was 2.45 per cent per annum. This is not particularly high by post-war European standards but it is more than what we observed, over the same period, in countries like Sweden (2.35 per cent), the US (2.2 per cent), the UK (2.05 per cent) and Switzerland (0.8 per cent) which also have fairly independent central banks. It was even more than in Denmark and Norway although central bank independence is very weak in these countries.

The European Central Bank had announced that it wanted to keep the average inflation rate in the eurozone below 2 per cent. It has not kept its promise – neither in 2001 nor in 2002 nor in 2003. These failures are due to the ECB's monetary policy.

The lowering of the main financing rate in April 1999 was a clear mistake, and it took the European Central Bank far too long to correct it. When the eurozone economy overheated in 2000, the ECB reacted by raising the main financing rate by 1.75 percentage points. It then turned around reducing the main financing rate in May 2001 – one year before the beginning of an unusual series of scheduled national elections within the eurozone (in the Netherlands, Ireland, France, Germany, Finland, Belgium, Austria, Spain, Greece). I have shown that the governments of these countries commanded, and still command, a majority in the Governing Council of the European Central Bank.[5] More precisely, a majority of the ECB Council members comes from these countries and, at the same time, is associated with one of the parties in government.

The European Central Bank has not only announced an inflation target but also a reference rate for monetary expansion (4.5 per cent per annum for M3). Up to now, it has exceeded this reference rate in every single year: M3 grew at a rate of 5.7 per cent in 1999, 4.9 per cent in 2000, 5.5 per cent in 2001, 7.2 per cent in 2002 and 7.1 per cent in 2003. If the ECB had kept monetary expansion in 1999 and 2000 at 4.5 per cent, the inflation rate in 2001 and 2002 would have been reduced by about 0.8 percentage points. With a rate of approximately 1.65 per cent, inflation would have stayed within the ECB's inflation target. At least, this is what the long-run quantity theory of money would predict.

In May 2003, the Governing Council of the European Central Bank changed its strategy. It has raised the inflation target, and it has delegated the reference rate for monetary expansion to second rank among its indicators. The inflation rate is now to be kept close to, but below, 2 per cent. This is something of a joke reminiscent of the worst excesses of Brussels diplomacy. A target inflation rate of 1.999 . . . per cent?

On the assumptions explicitly stated by the ECB, the monetary reference rate of 4.5 per cent has implied an inflation target of 1.0–2.0

per cent with the mid-point at 1.5 per cent.[6] Thus, the inflation brakes that had originally been installed to restrain monetary policy are being gradually weakened. At the same time, the European Stability and Growth Pact was broken in 2003 and there are plans to soften the limits on government budget deficits.

Moreover, changes in the composition of the ECB Council will lead to a more inflationary policy stance. When the members of the ECB Council were appointed in June 1998, the conservative German government of the day insisted on appointing conservatives to the Board of Executive Directors for the European Central Bank. The only socialist among the six executive directors was Wim Duisenberg, a monetary hardliner. The government of Helmut Kohl enjoyed an extremely strong bargaining position because the decision had to be unanimous and because Germany was asked to sacrifice its monetary leadership. Without German assent, EMU would not have started. In the future, EMU will persist regardless of whether there is agreement on the appointment of new executive directors. If necessary, the European Central Bank could be run by a Governing Council consisting exclusively of the national central bank governors. This means that the government that most closely shares the inflation preferences of the median national central bank governor will have the strongest bargaining power.[7]

There can be no doubt that the inflation rate preferred by the median central bank governor is considerably higher than the inflation rate preferred by the German Kohl government.[8] Thus, we should expect that, gradually, monetary conservatives on the Executive Board will be replaced by more inflation-prone central bankers until the median of the Governing Council coincides with the median among the national central bank governors.

From 2006 onwards, the ten new member states, eight of them East European countries, will become eligible to join the eurozone. Most of them have already declared that they want to join the eurozone as soon as possible. We know from the 1990s that it is not very difficult to satisfy the convergence criteria for entering the eurozone during as short a period as two years. The inflation record of the East European countries, even recently, has been disastrous. It indicates that their aversion to inflation is very weak. Their representatives on the Governing Council of the European Central Bank are likely to shift the balance towards substantially higher inflation.

To some extent, however, this effect will be mitigated by the fact that the relative prices of their goods tend to rise *vis-à-vis* eurozone goods. This is due to the strong productivity growth in their export sectors which raises the prices of non-tradable goods relative to tradable goods. Thus, once these countries have joined the eurozone, they will experience much higher inflation than the other members.

We must also take into account that when Poland and the Baltic states in particular join the eurozone the Swedish economy will become more open *vis-à-vis* the eurozone.

For Sweden, as for anybody else, the decision to join the eurozone would be irreversible. According to the European treaties, no country may leave the eurozone unless that country leaves the European Union altogether. If the decision is risky and if the Swedes want to keep their options open, they can only do this by postponing the decision. The irreversibility of joining strengthens the case for a 'wait-and-see' policy.

In the end, the decision to join or not to join is about more than just monetary policy, inflation and employment. European Monetary Union is the stepping stone for the centralization of many other economic policies and, ultimately, for the founding of a European state. Centralization reduces the cost of information and the cost of dealing with international spillovers. But it also reduces diversity and political competition. It suppresses international differences in preferences and gives the state more power over the citizens. This is the political dimension of the EMU decision.

Notes

1. R. Vaubel, 'Real Exchange-Rate Changes in the European Community: A New Approach to the Determination of Optimum Currency Areas', *Journal of International Economics*, 8, 1978, pp. 319–39; and 'Monetary Integration Theory', in Zis, G., Vaubel, R., Baker, S., Hitiris, T. and Peera, N. (eds), *International Economics (Surveys in Economics)*, London, New York: Longman, 1988, pp. 223–62.
2. R. Vaubel, 'The Future of the Euro: A Public Choice Perspective', in F. Capie and G. Wood (eds), *Monetary Unions*, London: Routledge, 2003, pp. 146–81.
3. *Ibid.*
4. V. Winschel, 'EMU Enlargement', Paper presented at the Annual Conference of the German Economic Association, Magdeburg, October 2001.
5. Vaubel, 'The Future of the Euro', tables 6.5 and 6.6.

6. The reference rate for monetary expansion has been derived from the quantity-theoretic equation

$$\Delta p = \Delta m - \Delta y + \Delta v$$

where Δp is the inflation rate, Δm is the rate of monetary expansion, Δy is the real growth rate of the economy and Δv is the rate of change of velocity. The ECB has declared that it assumes $\Delta y = 2.0$ to 2.5 and $\Delta v = -0.5$ to -1.0. If $\Delta m = 4.5$, the equation implies an inflation target of 1.0–2.0 per cent with a mid-point of 1.5 per cent.
7. Vaubel, 'The Future of the Euro'.
8. Compare also the national 'sensitivities to inflation' estimated by B. Hayo 'Inflation, Culture, Central Bank Independence and Price Stability', *European Journal of Political Economy*, vol. 14, 1998, pp. 241–63. from opinion poll data.

7
The UK and the Euro: Politics versus Economics in a Long-Run Perspective

James Foreman-Peck

The successful launch of the euro at the beginning of 2002 also re-floated the question of the future membership of Britain, Denmark and Sweden. Denmark had obtained an exemption from joining the euro after voters initially rejected the Maastricht Treaty in June 1992. A referendum to determine whether Denmark should join the single currency, held in September 2000, declined the euro by 53 to 47 per cent. Before the poll took place, the independent advisory council of Danish economists reported to the government that the issue was 'linked more to political considerations than economic factors.' They did not expect the economic advantages to be very significant and were agnostic as to whether such advantages would be offset by the costs of permanently abandoning an independent monetary policy.[1]

Sweden joined the EU in 1995 with no exemption from adopting the euro. The Swedish government announced in January 2002 the intention to hold a referendum the following year. In May 2002, the European Commission stated that Sweden was not ready to join the euro because its currency was too unstable and the central bank was not independent enough from the government. Subsequently, opinion polls showed support for the euro waning, probably because Swedish performance outside the euro appeared to be better than the eurozone's. The date for the Swedish referendum has now been set for 14 September 2003.

The United Kingdom, under a Conservative government, negotiated an exemption from joining the euro in the Maastricht Treaty. The present Labour government is committed to the principle of joining

97

the single currency, unlike the Conservative opposition. However, the conditions that must be satisfied for joining raise the question as to whether there is much difference in substance between the two parties' policies. A Labour government decision to enter the euro is dependent on whether there is a clear and unambiguous economic case for membership, as defined by the Treasury's five economic tests. This condition virtually allows the Chancellor of the Exchequer, as Treasury minister, the power of veto over entry, for he determines whether the tests are satisfied. If and when the tests are passed so that 'the economic conditions for joining are right', the government is committed to holding a referendum. On 9 June 2003, the government published the assessment of the five economic tests, 18 supporting studies and the third outline national changeover plan. In effect, the judgement was 'not yet', though the presentation was more positive in view of the pro-euro stance of the Prime Mininster.[2]

A major consideration in referenda for all three countries will be the perceived political future of the Europe that the euro serves; a 'United States of Europe' or a loose federation of nation states. Entry for all three candidates would be much easier in the second case. But there may be differences between candidates even so; one judgement was that the chances of Denmark and Sweden joining European Monetary Union by 2006 or 2007 were significantly above 50 per cent but for the UK they were significantly below 50 per cent.[3]

Rather than attempt to predict, this study aims to set out the economic issues that determine the desirability of British euro entry and how they came about. The following section gives some of the historical and economic background to Britain's engagement with Europe. The second section briefly outlines the ambiguities of the British government's position on euro entry and the third section describes the poll evidence on the paradoxical state of British public opinion. The fourth and fifth sections analyze respectively the principal economic benefits and costs of the euro. The sixth section takes a longer-term view about how the eurozone might evolve and the changes it is likely to bring about.

Britain's engagement with Europe

Britain is often accused of being a 'half-hearted European' (perhaps suspected, by other countries, of hankering after an imperial past), joining schemes for integration, such as the euro, only when too late to exercise any influence over the relevant institutions. There is a less perjorative interpretation, one that also carries wider implications for European integration; Britain has, for much of the time, seen the European 'project' only as economic policy, to be judged in these terms against what the British economy requires.

Monetary background

A long history of a national currency, for a considerable period soundly managed, created a predisposition to regard change as unnecessary. For this reason Britain remained aloof from the 1867 International Monetary Conference's proposal for a world currency.[4] On the other hand, a decade ago the most recent half-century looked very much less creditable.

The pound sterling that would be abandoned with euro membership, originated as a specific weight of silver of a specified fineness, perhaps as early as the 8th century, and certainly by the 11th. In the 19th-century heyday (or perhaps prime) British currency was actually defined in terms of gold. Giving up the precious metal link after 1945 relaxed the constraint on monetary policy, and the floating sterling exchange rate that followed provided even less discipline.[5] With the abandonment of any precious metal underpinning, trust in sterling and monetary policy after World War II was reflected in the foreign exchange value, which fell from $4.03 to $1.70 by 1976, while inflation peaked at an annual rate of 26.9 per cent in August of the previous year.[6]

A variety of tactics to create monetary stability has been tried since 1945, including shadowing the Deutschmark and monetary targeting. Ironically, one of the greater political humiliations for sterling, being forced out of the European Exchange Rate Mechanism in 1992, marked the beginning of the present convergence of the British economy to a stable non-inflationary growth path.

The turn around in post-war British economic policy began with Margaret Thatcher's government, elected in 1979. In addition to a series of monetary policy experiments, a variety of structural reforms in the economy were begun, including privatization and steps to increase labour market flexibility. Inflation receded along with unemployment (eventually) and economic growth resumed.

The Conservative Party's long period of office eventually forced radical change upon the opposition Labour Party; abandonment of a

commitment to socialist economic management, such as national-
ization. Election of the 'New Labour' government of 1997, therefore,
saw no break in the principles of national economic management.
Indeed, the government was aware that to convince financial markets
that they were not 'old socialists' they were obliged to be 'more royalist
than the king'. Most astutely, they immediately returned independence
to the Bank of England. They also created an independent Monetary
Policy Committee mandated to follow a symmetric inflation rule and
to report their deliberations.

These arrangements at last are generally reckoned to provide best
practice monetary policy. For instance, co-ordination between independent monetary and fiscal policies is far easier for Britain under
the present arrangements than for eurozone[7] with its many national
taxing and spending policies. Not only are the monetary policy
strategy and inflation target of the European Central Bank (ECB)
criticized for being unsatisfactory and possibly damaging to the
ECB's credibility: unless the mechanisms for interest rate setting are
rethought, there are also risks that inappropriate decisions will be
taken after eurozone enlargement with up to 27 member states.[8]

For the better management of the nation's finances, the Chancellor
of the Exchequer introduced the long overdue distinction between
capital and current account spending. Borrowing to enhance the
nation's productive capital stock was acceptable, as was temporary
borrowing to stabilize the economy in the face of shocks. To ensure
government debt increases were restricted to these two purposes, he
accepted two obligations on government policy; that current account
spending should balance tax receipts over the cycle and that the
government debt to national income ratio should not exceed (the
admittedly arbitrary ratio of) 40 per cent.

These innovations in the British macroeconomic management framework are substantial achievements – certainly superior to the present
equivalent institutions of the eurozone, the European Central Bank
and the Stability and Growth Pact. Where the government now
needs to make comparable advances is in the fields of the health
service, education and transport, about which there is widespread
dissatisfaction among the electorate. In these services, there is much
to be learned from other European countries, but joining the euro
and possible consequent closer political integration with Europe do
not promise to address British concerns.

European integration

What Britain has reasonably wanted from the rest of Europe, historically, is simply free trade, not imported institutions designed to address continental problems. The first institution of the present remarkable phase of European integration was the European Coal and Steel Community. This proved an effective method of depoliticizing conflict over iron ore and coal deposits that had exercised France and Germany over the preceding 70 years. But it was just irrelevant to the British coal and steel industries that were quite independent of the industrial belt of the Ruhr, Belgium and Northern France. Economic geography ensured that there was no economic case for British participation in laying this particular historical ghost. [9]

British trade connections and investment were substantially intercontinental in the 19th century; Britain's largest trading partners were the United States and India in the 1850s, and by the end of the century the majority of British emigrants were heading for Australasia. The commitments forged by these relationships almost inevitably created difficulties for Britain in accepting the higher trade barrier consequences of the common external tariff agenda favoured by the 1955 Spaak Committee. Britain naturally favoured a free trade area that would not have these effects, rather than a customs union. So she did not sign up to the Treaty of Rome in 1957, and formed instead the European Free Trade Area, with Sweden among others, as an interim institution.[10]

The Common Agricultural Policy (CAP), another legacy of history at the heart of the European Union, for some time proved unacceptable to Britain. Britain industrialized earlier than the rest of Europe, became highly urbanized by the middle of the 19th century and committed to free trade liberalism. As a consequence, the agricultural sector was allowed to contract, in marked contrast to France and Germany. These countries resisted the influx of cheap 'New World' produce with higher tariff barriers.[11] Britain possessed a small, highly efficient agricultural sector by the 1950s (albeit subsidized, supposedly because of the experience of war-time blockade). France and Germany still employed large numbers of people in low-productivity agriculture. The CAP, designed to keep up food prices in order to protect the agricultural sector, would be (and is) extremely expensive for Britain as a net food importer.[12] Reform, announced in June 2003, will not cut the financial cost of the policy but merely reduce the damage both in terms of unwanted production and to the rest of the world, by way of preparation for the forthcoming World Trade Organization negotiations.

The politics of European Monetary Union

Monetary union also is a solution to a Franco-German political problem rather than an altruistic device for advancing the economic interests of Europe as a whole. The euro is only one means of achieving the greater exchange rate stability sought by those concerned to advance European integration. Greater co-ordination within the Exchange Rate Mechanism framework could have delivered the same, and was indeed considered for this purpose. Monetary union was chosen instead as part of a Franco-German deal over German reunification. The Deutschmark was traded in for a unified state. This large, united Germany needed to be acceptable to France, and monetary union was the price charged by the French government.[13]

Essentially, the French (and much of the rest of Western Europe) felt they had been obliged to dance to the *Bundesbank*'s monetary tune. Yet they lacked any influence over the *Bundesbank*'s constitution or behaviour, directed primarily to domestic German goals. Monetary union would end German leadership in a significant area of policy and give France more control. Despite *Bundesbank* and popular opposition, the German government was prepared to make this concession because the Franco-German relationship was a top priority.

France also wanted a wide monetary union to provide counterweights to the Germans. Since politics led economics, 'optimum currency area' arguments that suggested a smaller zone – of the type originally favoured by the *Bundesbank*, consisting of France, West Germany and Benelux – were ignored.

Pressure that would be exerted by monetary union for fiscal co-ordination and greater European fiscal powers was acceptable. Such extension of economic powers would require more European government. As far as France was concerned, political union was also necessary for one of her prime concerns, German foreign policy transparency. Again, European economics was a tool of European politics.

Against this background, the British and Danish opt-outs as well as the forthcoming Swedish referendum are entirely understandable. Why should an interest rate set in Frankfurt happen to suit the needs of their economies? They did not need the externally imposed financial disciplines that Italy and Spain appreciated. Nor were the issues central to the Franco-German deal of so much concern to them. Britain could not have been both more central to this arrangement and pursued its economic interests. Monetary union in 1999 was not a desirable economic policy for Britain, with its highly developed and internationalized financial markets. Only if politics was to have priority over economics for Britain as well was participation necessary.

Britain's apparently less than wholehearted historical commitment to European integration, therefore, should not be understood as mere obstruction. The hand dealt by economic history is different for Britain than for the core countries. Where monetary union is concerned this is also true. In addition to the monetary institutions established recently, financial development over centuries has made Britain significantly different from France and Germany and to ignore the legacy of history would be both expensive and unnecessary. Almost certainly, such national or regional differences will be relevant to some other European countries as well.

British domestic politics

Why, then, is Britain even considering a euro referendum? Prime Minister Tony Blair believes that 'our future lies in Europe'. According to the British Treasury (web site), 'The determining factor underpinning any government decision on membership of the single currency is the national economic interest.' But at the same time, the present British government is 'in favour of UK membership of EMU'.

Chancellor Gordon Brown for some years has maintained that the costs or benefits to the economy are a constraint upon policy, by requiring that his five tests first be satisfied. The tests are:

1. sustainable convergence between Britain and the economies of a single currency;
2. whether there is sufficient flexibility to cope with economic change;
3. the effect on investment;
4. the impact on our financial services industry;
5. whether it is good for employment.

Implicitly, he has contended that it is not worth paying anything for whatever political advantages if any accrue from euro membership. He has divided a unitary decision into two stages: someone who believed the political consequences of the euro were significant would, to some extent, be prepared to override the 'national economic interest'.

Even if the true net costs/benefits to the economy of joining the euro could be firmly established for any particular date, electorates and government ministers might disagree about entry, simply because they evaluated differently the political advantages or drawbacks of euro membership. The value of membership of, and contributing to, a politically integrated Europe, providing a counterweight to the US in world affairs, might be judged worth a slightly lower economic growth rate. On the other hand, an electorate might conclude that a slightly smaller income than possible is a price worth paying for maintaining political independence from a bureaucratic European super-state to which the euro inevitably leads. In these cases, the economics of the euro, even when certain, are not decisive but could simply indicate the 'price' of a policy.

Clearly, timing and conditions of entry do affect the economic interest; joining the euro at too high a sterling rate would damage industry and employment unnecessarily. From inception, the euro fell against sterling and only in the last year began to rise. Hence the debate about the extent to which the pound is currently overvalued against the euro has been animated.[14] Germany is still suffering from locking in to the euro at an uncompetitive exchange rate and would be further damaged if Britain entered at an undervalued rate. One estimate is that £0.68 is appropriate (the rate on 21 May 2003 was £0.71). £0.68 makes France's GDP slightly bigger than Britain's, and so is acceptable to France. British manufacturing industry, of course, prefers a lower rate, that is, more pence to buy one euro. The National Institute of Economic Research currently sees no major problems associated with joining EMU at around 1.50 euros to the pound (£0.66). They recognize that there are risks to the UK if the euro appreciates against the dollar after entry but consider there to be offsets in the medium term.[15]

If the government announces a credible rate together with a date for entry the market will ensure sterling converges on that rate. This is what seems to have happened when Britain returned to the gold standard in 1925. Unfortunately, the exchange rate in such circumstances cannot be taken as the 'equilibrium' rate, driven as it is by market perceptions of government policy.

However problematic is choosing the entry rate, there is more at stake in the government's position. For some, such as the Prime Minister, the politics mean it is merely a matter of timing and terms. The five tests could amount to more than this, however. If they were never to be satisfied, the government would be announcing, in effect, both that they favoured euro membership and that they could not join because it was against the national economic interest for the forsee-able future. So, for others, the economics may be a real bar. For a third group, the five tests were an ingenious ploy to prevent the govern-ment tearing itself apart over the euro, and indeed to avoid wider public debate ('kicking the issue into the long grass'). Monetary union then becomes a technical exercise, subject to a referendum, that requires an as yet unspecified majority in favour, when and if the government sees fit to make the recommendation. Whether 'the conditions are right' potentially becomes a political 'let out' if the government thinks they would lose a referendum – or perhaps even an opportunity to avoid a split within the government.

Public opinion

Public opinion, even if softening a little at the time of the introduction of the euro, is hardly enthusiastic.[16] Subsequently, it has become more opposed. Much, of course, depends upon how the questions are phrased in the opinion poll and whether a particular stratum of the population is addressed. The general result is that a majority do not favour joining the euro, but at the same time they expect Britain to enter in the next decade.[17]

On one reading, the polls tells us something intriguing about the British psyche or British politics. Voters appear to feel powerless to prevent a policy of the government that they have elected. Alternatively, they do not trust their own present judgement and expect to change their current views, once government starts campaigning for the euro in earnest.

Businessmen, as exporters to eurozone, prefer the certainty that currency stability within the euro would bring. One poll in early 2002 showed that after a decline over the previous three years, belief among 'business leaders' in the value of the euro to Britain had risen.[18] By around 3:2, Britain's business leaders supported rather than opposed Britain joining. But, furthermore, they like lower exchange rates and dislike higher. So the recent appreciation of the euro may have helped move euro entry down their agenda. A year later, a survey of 164 chairman and chief executives found 50 per cent of them opposed 'in principle' to British membership of the single currency and only 42 per cent in favour. This was the first time the annual 'captains of industry' study showed a majority against the euro.

Like the Swedish electorate, the British as a whole may have been swayed by the divergent fortunes of their own currency area and the eurozone over the period since the introduction of the euro. Staying out certainly did not seem to have wreaked any damage – economic growth, unemployment, inflation and budget deficits were all better than eurozone averages. Foreign investment was up by a half and one-third originated in the eurozone. The euro was more volatile against the dollar than sterling and UK long interest rates were below those of the eurozone, even though short rates were above.

Whatever the reason, a poll in early May 2003 showed an increased majority of people in Britain (58 per cent) against the euro. Contrary to previous indications, a strong government push for the euro would apparently boost the numbers against it.

Opinion polls indicate what people believe to be the case – which is helpful for predicting and explaining behaviour – but they do not tell us whether their beliefs are correct. Nor do opinion polls tell us about the intensity of beliefs and, in particular, whether responses would be translated into turn-out at a referendum. How will the euro affect the British economy?

Economic benefits of the euro

Despite negative public opinion the benefits of British euro membership are often contended to outweigh the key costs.[19] There are four widely alleged principal economic gains from EMU:

- reduction in expense of changing currency;
- a cut in exchange risk, stimulating greater trade and foreign investment with the rest of Europe, and
- lowering the risk-premium in the cost of raising capital;
- increased transparency in price comparisons, enhancing competition.

Money changing costs

The legacy of history that conferred on Britain a sophisticated and widely spread banking system thereby also guarantees that the gross gains from a reduction in the currency changing cost are small. Most euro and pound exchanges are made within the banking system – by credit card, for instance. Because of computerization, they do not consume resources whatever currency is used. Only transactions by hand – tourist exchanges, for example – are really affected. Analysis of the reduction in these costs shows the net gains, if any, are small and depend critically on the discount rate.

The gains for Britain amount to about 0.1 per cent of GDP annually, about £1 billion per year.[20] Against this annual sum must be set a large one-off cost in the means of changing the pound into euros – including modifying vending machines, accounting systems and the banks' high street machines. A reasonable central estimate of the changeover cost is £30 billion.[21]

Comparing the £1 billion per annum benefits in perpetuity with the one-off £30 billion cost requires a discount rate

$$\frac{£1\,\text{billion}}{x} <> £30 \text{ billion}$$

where x is the real discount rate. Until the beginning of this year x = 6 per cent, the official Treasury rate for cost–benefit analysis, euro transactions benefits are £16.67 billion < £30 billion costs. The policy is undesirable on economic grounds. The rate has now been reduced radically to x = 3.5 per cent yielding benefits of £28.7 billion < £30 billion costs.

In both cases, there are negative net benefits from a policy with other profound implications (and anyway the benefits are overstated because exchange costs are likely to fall with the passage of time and the advance of technology).

Reducing exchange rate risk

The period since World War II saw a continuously rising proportion of trade conducted with Europe. By now, history has created a pattern of British trade and investment which divides as roughly half with Europe (the euro area) and half with the wider world (the dollar area). Dollar trade and investment is not necessarily with the United States because so many other international transactions are denominated in dollars and so many other economies link directly or indirectly to the dollar. British dollar investment is with the US and Far East, whereas trade is more with Europe. Forty-one per cent of British foreign income originates in the euro area when investment is included, while three-quarters of incoming investment to Britain originates outside the EU. Will joining the euro really reduce exchange risk on these transactions?

One way of thinking about the question is to assume, not implausibly, that the Deutschmark would have been the dominating element in the behaviour of the euro, had it existed before 1999. The hypothetical euro/dollar exchange rate then obtained back to 1980 is highly variable. Moreover, the principal sources of variability have not been removed. Eurozone and the US continue to prefer different approaches to regulating the supply side of the economy ('flexibility' versus 'co-determination') encouraging swings in market sentiment about future performance. There are still differences in business cycles between the currency zones that cause fluctuations in interest rates and Europe's typically slower rate of adoption of new technologies persists.

Although inflation differentials have almost been eliminated, this is no new development. At least a decade and a half's experience has not reduced very large variations in the exchange rate. The other factors listed above continue to affect the 'real exchange rate' (the exchange rate adjusted for relative inflation).

Recent history has already demonstrated the dangers for sterling. Between 1988 and 1992 Britain first shadowed and then tied to the Deutschmark (the equivalent now would be the euro). As German reunification led to a large appreciation of the Deutschmark against the dollar, the pound fluctuated substantially. After Britain left the ERM in 1992 the Deutschmark continued to appreciate against the dollar until 1995, when it began to fall. The successor euro from January 1999 has depreciated further. Over the same period sterling did not fluctuate so much. If Britain joined the euro, exchange risk against the dollar would increase as the euro, oscillates. Outside the euro, the pound can average the two rates. We must conclude that there would not necessarily be any reduction in exchange risk from joining the euro and possibly the risk would increase.

Does exchange risk matter very much anyway for Britain? By and large it does not, because the economy and the financial sector are sufficiently large and sophisticated to diversify most risk away. If the

British economy is well run, monetary policy and a flexible supply side will be able to minimize the impact of general turbulence in the world economy.

Lower cost of capital

Would joining the euro lower the British cost of capital? Capital moves across borders in search of quick profits, and in so doing equalizes the British real interest rate with those in the rest of the world. The dollar interest rate is a good approximation to the 'world rate', plus a risk-premium reflecting the volatility of the exchange rate. So long as the British economy is well managed, exchange risk consequent upon such volatility will be small. The cost of capital will be at world market rates and joining the euro cannot cut the rate below that level.[22]

Greater price transparency

The 'greater price transparency' argument is just mistaken. It confuses transparency either with exchange risk, already discussed, or with restraints on competition. Closer inspection of Belgian and British car price differentials confirms that the cost of calculating the difference in two currencies is close to zero. What has prevented price convergence for so long is nothing to do with transparency and everything to do with restrictive agreements among car dealers.

The economic costs of the euro

Against these supposed benefits must be weighed three main economic costs:

- the destabilizing impact of shocks without the independent interest rate and exchange rate stabilizers;
- the effects of 'harmonization' initiatives triggered by EMU; and
- a possible commitment to supporting a euro countries with financial problems, especially those arising from state pension deficits.

Destabilizing shocks

As already noted, adopting the euro means also joining a zone with a single interest rate. Capital movements between countries ensure this is so. Only if there were exchange controls or differential taxes on interest rates – explicitly forbidden under the Maastricht Treaty – could it be otherwise. It is this 'one size fits all' monetary policy that is the principal economic cost of euro membership. If there is a slump in one country, a lower interest rate is appropriate there to encourage economic activity. Yet in the eurozone, this is only possible if other major economies also experience the same negative shock. Otherwise economies unaffected by the slump would be subject to inflationary pressures.

A common interest rate in Britain and in the rest of the eurozone would not destabilize the UK economy very much if Britain and the eurozone constituted an 'optimal currency area'. If they did, one or more of the following conditions would hold:

- Shocks would have similar impacts – be 'symmetric', perhaps because industries are similar, because the economies have a similar structure, or because they have a comparable trade pattern.[23]
- When a shock strikes there would be strong fiscal compensation mechanisms – an adversely affected region pays less taxes, gets more benefit payments and may receive special regional assistance.
- High labour mobility would dampen the impact of shocks; a region performing well draws in workers unemployed in regions doing badly.
- Wages would be highly responsive; a region hit by a severe shock causing unemployment lowers its wages and prices, while other regions raise theirs. Employment then begins to recover in the lower-wage region and contract in regions that now have higher wages.

These conditions are the concern of the first two of the Chancellor's tests. They are not met for Britain and the eurozone and will not be for the foreseeable future on unchanged policies.

To see how much the independent interest rate policy instrument can matter, imagine what would have happened had there been a euro when the Great Depression of 1929–33 struck. The deflation of the German economy by Chancellor Bruening between 1929 and 1931 has affinities with the economic consequences of German reunification in the 1990s, and there is now some concern about the possibility of price deflation in Germany, encouraged by the example of Japan.

The EMU counterfactual supposes that when the World Depression struck, there were:

1. only one discount rate policy for France, Germany and the UK;
2. permanently fixed exchange rates between these economies but a floating exchange rate with the United States; and
3. all four economies continued to pursue independent fiscal policies without co-operation.

A common European currency would have precisely these consequences. The counterfactual is then evaluated by imposing these assumptions in an econometric model of the inter-war economy.[24]

With only one European monetary policy, the best approach is to address the problems of Germany, then the economy in the most dire straits. This policy was less suitable for the other countries whose problems were different. Their national fiscal policies therefore needed to be more active but at the same time more competitive. Abandoning one policy instrument, national discount rates, Europe (Britain, France and Germany in this model) is much worse off than when both fiscal and monetary instruments are employed ideally by each country. Despite being the focus of European monetary policy, in this scenario Germany continues to suffer the greatest output (and implicitly employment) collapse in Europe. European monetary union is bad for the United States as well in these circumstances. Europe exports unemployment to the US by depreciating the 'euro' exchange rate. Even with ideal policies, shocks comparable to those of the World Depression are very damaging with monetary union.

The effects are much more muted in a scenario in which all four economies had left the gold standard in 1929 and floated their exchange rates, the position corresponding to the pre-ERM state of affairs. Europe would have performed far better (again comparing optimum policies between regimes), simply because there were more policy tools. The United Kingdom (the most open economy) received the greatest benefit from the less constrained policy that allowed national exchange rate and interest movements.

Thanks to the widely held and substantial variable interest rate mortgage in Britain, we can be sure that today, as in 1929, there will be different responses to monetary shocks by the British economy from those of France and Germany. Although introduction of fixed-rate long-term mortgages may reduce the interest responsiveness of the British consumers' expenditure relative to those of the eurozone, they will not eliminate the problem because many Britons will still prefer the apparently cheaper variable-rate mortgage.[25]

HM Treasury's latest study reinforced this point by considering what would have happened if Britain had joined EMU in 1999 at the same time as the 11 'first wave' members.[26] The exercise indicated that the economy would have experienced greater economic instability of output, inflation and interest rates than it did. Moreover, these effects would not have been merely transitory; output growth would have stabilized only after a decade and inflation would have continued to be more erratic permanently.

Harmonization

The eurozone has neither the wage flexibility nor the high labour mobility that become more necessary under monetary union with the abandonment of national interest rate policies. Other (expensive) policy instruments – fiscal, industrial, regional – must therefore be used more intensively to maintain the same level of economic activity. Rather than explicitly acknowledging this fact, there is instead pressure for 'harmonization' of taxes and other institutions. Harmonization will build up central federal institutions that would ultimately acquire the power to spend and tax in regions struck by asymmetric shocks. This policy does not provide any help for EMU but is a springboard to greater powers in Brussels that could.

Possible consequences of this strategy can be exposed by another argument by historical analogy. The long persistent Italian Mezzogiorno problem is a consequence of premature or otherwise inappropriate monetary unification and harmonization of two very different regions in 1860. Had Garibaldi turned to fight the French in the North instead of heading for Naples after his first victorious campaign, Italian economic and political history could have been very different. In the preceding century, Naples was by far the largest city in Italy, and one of the biggest in the world, reflecting relatively high economic development in the region. Yet, as a consequence of Garibaldi's enthusiasm, the South stagnated relative to the North. Without monetary and political union in 1860 the South would probably have developed faster. A nation was formally created at the expense of prosperity and cohesion. Over the 25 years before 1990 alone, the Mezzogiorno received 20–30 per cent of output from the rest of Italy with no noticeable effect on regional income differentials.[27] The transfers and harmonization merely encouraged the persistence of inappropriate wage levels.

The durability of Italian monetary union was due to political unification and there is other historical evidence that links political unification and lasting monetary unions. It includes the Scandinavian monetary union that broke down in 1918 without political union, and the contrasting England–Scotland monetary link, permanently secured by a common monarch and parliament in 1707.

Financial rescues for other eurozone members

A monetary union is usually at risk from fiscal profligacy of one member at the expense of others. In the late 19th-century Latin Monetary Union, it was Italy, with its refusal to curtail silver coinage, that took advantage of the leader, France.[28] Now, the three largest nations in the eurozone, Germany, France and Italy, have serious projected state pension deficits. In 1996 they were predicted to reach respectively about 10 per cent, 8 per cent and 11 per cent of GDP by 2030.[29] In total these prospective deficits amount to more than one-third of the British national income. Since then, Germany and Italy have taken some steps to reduce their expected deficits but France has taken none. Meanwhile, slower economic growth and rising unemployment has increased the vulnerability of all three countries.

Any state running a budget deficit (for instance, to pay for pensions) must borrow and in a monetary union this raises the union interest rate. This higher borrowing cost spills over to other union states, as they have to increase the interest payments to service their debts. All states then must reduce their planned government spending as resources are diverted to the increased interest payments. This reasoning led to the restrictions in the Maastricht Treaty of a maximum budget deficit of 3 per cent of GDP and a maximum debt of 60 per cent of GDP. Fines were to be imposed if countries broke the Pact, of 0.2–0.5 per cent of GDP. Unfortunately fines would increase a country's problems at a time when it is probably suffering from a recession, so the Pact lacks credibility if enough members are affected. The Stability

Pact is not sufficient protection for Britain from a continental 'pensions meltdown'.

The Pact may constrain individual countries wishing to employ fiscal policy to stabilize their economies, although the fiscal framework of EMU has not succeeded in safeguarding fiscal discipline, especially in the large member states.[30] But it is unlikely to prevent a bail-out in this case because state pensions can be treated as an off-budget item, provided other EMU members connive. If they do, the resulting debt can accumulate, so long as the 60 per cent Maastricht maximum national debt to income ratio is treated as less of a binding obligation than the deficit limit.

The risk of even some of these pension liabilities becoming a charge on the UK taxpayer is a serious economic concern with regard to entering EMU, especially given the experience with the Common Agricultural Policy.

Institutional yardstick competition and institutional change

Neither the economic nor the political consequences of euro membership will ever be crystal clear. Indeed whether or not the UK joins could influence the development of the eurozone. It has been maintained that Britain missed out on the opportunity to influence the CAP by not joining the Common Market on formation and will do so again with the euro.[31]

This contention is the opposite of the truth. By staying out and preserving and creating well-functioning institutions such as the Monetary Policy Committee and the pre-1973 agricultural policy, a country such as Britain can provide a demonstration or yardstick. This will be more powerful than a single vote among many around tables where a variety of political issues are in play.[32] As we have discussed, in both the euro and agricultural policy cases European policy was formed by a Franco-German rapprochement. The CAP was established to protect French agriculture in exchange for German industrial access to French markets. Similarly, the euro was agreed to allow more French control of European monetary policy than under the *Bundesbank* in return for French acceptance of German reunification. Britain was irrelevant to these bilateral deals and could not have influenced them. It proved convenient for some other states with close economic and political ties to these two countries, or for historical reasons of their own, to follow. But there is no reason this should be so for the whole of Europe.

The rise of Europe at the time that the older civilization and economy of China was stagnating stemmed in large part from the variety of administrations in Europe in contrast to monolithic China.[33] There was yardstick competition between nations and more opportunity for innovations, technological and institutional, to be tested without state repression.[34] Whenever a reforming European government came to power, enquiries were made as to what useful developments could be taken from other European countries. In due course the Japanese Meiji government adopted this line as well, borrowing their education system from Germany, their telegraphy from France and their navy from Britain. A monolithic, corporate Europe, led by the euro, will cut out this source of vitality.

Will the eurozone eventually become an optimal currency area because of institutional reform? In particular will the eurozone ever introduce the flexibility necessary to make a monetary union work well? If existing members of the union were rational, exclusively economic, agents they might aim to admit more flexible nations because newcomers could disproportionately absorb the adjustment costs of adverse shocks.[35] A rational economically motivated outsider would never want to join a union of members less flexible than itself because of the increased own adjustment costs. Once joined (perhaps for political reasons) there are incentives to become as inflexible as the most inflexible existing members precisely to avoid shouldering the burdens of adjustment. The incentives on individual states seem to pull in the opposite direction for the necessary institutional reforms.

A predictable institutional change is increasing powers for the European state, thanks to the dynamics of change within the single market and the monetary union. Single markets – the aspect of the European Union Britain traditionally most favours – require different characteristics (asymmetries) from monetary unions (symmetries) to work well. Advantages from trade depended upon differences between countries whereas successful monetary unions require similarities. US evidence suggests single markets encourage greater differences, greater specialization.[36] Greater specialization implies varied responses to a common monetary policy that will require the increasing use of other European state policy tools. The logic of institutional eurozone change does not therefore encourage those uninterested in a European super-state.

Conclusion

Britain has a very long tradition of national monetary and other policy independence. Although the half-century after World War II is not reckoned to have been a particularly successful example of economic management, the country recently has acquired good macroeconomic institutions that it would be hard to give up for less well-designed European structures. Equally, in domestic politics, since 1997 there has been some resolution of a century of ideologically based party conflict towards a more consensual approach in micro-economic management. The compulsion present in some other countries to acquire European-level institutions to resolve domestic conflicts is therefore absent in the British case. The principal European institutions – in particular the euro as a means of creating exchange rate stability – have been constructed to address Franco-German problems which are not identical with British concerns. It will therefore be no surprise to find that they do not necessarily fit British interests.

The British government's stated position is that the economic case for entering the eurozone has to be right, yet they are in favour of membership in principle. This has allowed a convenient ambiguity to persist. Is membership just a matter of timing and choosing the right entry exchange rate, because the political advantages are obvious? Or is it possible that the economic and/or other costs might just be too high? Public opinion polls reveal a similar ambiguity. All polls show a majority against joining now, but there is also a majority expecting to enter regardless of their preferences. Either the public is alienated from formal politics or willing to learn or both. But what is it to learn?

A systematic analysis of the economic costs and benefits of the euro concludes that the loss of an important policy instrument, the interest rate, together with greater rigidities imposed by a harmonization programme and possible sharing of other countries' pensions financial burdens are likely to outweigh the benefits. Because there is a trade-off between objectives there must be a political or evaluative element in the British choice of entry to the euro. However, the considerations relevant for Britain are very different from those motivating the core founders of the present monetary union, France and Germany. By remaining outside the euro Britain will maintain the freedom to develop and modify institutions from which Europe can learn. By entering, Britain will be caught up in an inexorable movement towards a European super-state over which she will have minimal influence and from which it will be difficult to extricate herself. There may be some lessons in Britain's circumstances for Sweden's euro decision.

Notes

1. The Danish currency is still participating in the Exchange Rate Mechanism (ERM-2) and is pegged within a 2.25 per cent band against the euro.
2. The assessment sets out 'the real benefits to Britain of membership of the single currency, shows that with the achievement of sustainable convergence and flexibility all five tests could and can be met, and lays down the concrete and practical steps which the Government will follow – radical steps which set out a new direction for reform, steps which set out the clear path ahead for Britain', *http://assessment.treasury.gov.uk/page_01.html*.
3. Credit Suisse, *Still cool, but warming up – Denmark, Sweden, UK and the euro*, July 2002, Zurich.
4. P.L. Cottrell, 'Silver Gold and the International Monetary Order 1851–96', in S.N. Broadberry and N.F.R. Crafts (eds), *Britain in the International Economy 1870–1939*, Cambridge: Cambridge University Press, 1992.
5. The link was abandoned in 1931 but an independent Bank of England, a deflationary international environment and perhaps a non-socialist government continued to be associated with broadly stable prices for the remaining years before World War II.
6. This limited period is what is referred to in the Treasury assessment (Introduction, para. 13) as 'the stop-go nature of the UK's economic history'.
7. A senior Treasury official regularly briefs the Bank of England Monetary Policy Committee about the Treasury's view of the future trajectory of the economy and the stance of fiscal policy.
8. P. De Grauwe, 'Challenges for Monetary Policy in Euroland', *Journal of Common Market Studies*, 40 (4), 2002, pp. 693–718.
9. For example, J. Foreman-Peck and G. Federico (eds), *European Industrial Policy: The Twentieth-Century Experience*, Oxford: Oxford University Press, 1999, chapter 15.
10. The tremendous damage suffered by New Zealand's economy from the 1970s, when Britain did eventually join, would probably have been even greater had Britain joined in the 1950s.
11. For example, M. Tracy, *Government and Agriculture in Western Europe 1880–1988*, New York: Harvester Wheatsheaf, 1989.
12. The average British family of four pays £16 a week in taxes and inflated prices to fund the CAP.

13. M. Levitt and C. Lord, *The Political Economy of European Monetary Union*, Basingstoke: Macmillan, 2000.
14. For example, *Financial Times*, 9 January 2002, p. 3.
15. R. Barrell, 'The UK and EMU: Choosing the Regime', *National Institute Economic Review*, 180, April 2002, pp. 54–71.
16. Some polls in early 2002 were: YouGov – *The Sunday Times*, 6 January; DHL – *The Independent*, 11 January; and NOP – *The Times*, 10 January.
17. 'Poll shows business turning on euro', Matthew Tempest, *The Guardian*, 20 January 2003.
18. MORI annual *Captains of Industry Survey*, 14 January 2002.
19. In this and the following section I draw substantially on work by Patrick Minford such as 'Should Britain join the euro – the Chancellor's five tests examined', *IEA Occasional Paper*, 126, September 2002.
20. European Commission 'One Market One Money – an Evaluation of the Potential Benefits and Costs of Forming an Economic and Monetary Union', *European Economy*, 44, October 1990.
21. House of Commons, 'What would the Euro cost British business?', *Trade and Industry Committee Report*, Cmnd HC755, 2000.
22. The euro will almost certainly obtain some of the seigniorage formerly accruing to the US dollar. People will hold euros rather than dollars as international exchange media, allowing Europeans to buy more from the rest of the world without paying with goods and services, as the Americans have formerly been able to do. But seigniorage gains are small compared with those of a prosperous and dynamic economy, which the euro could jeopardize.
23. Patrick Minford's more sophisticated econometric exercise on more recent data is contained in his 'Tests 1 and 2: flexibility and the costs in economic variability', in J. Bush (ed.) *The Economic Case against the Euro. New Europe for the No Campaign*, 2001 (downloadable at www.no-euro.com).
24. The model is described in J. Foreman-Peck, A. Hughes Hallett and Y. Ma, 'A Monthly Econometric Model of the Transmission of the Great Depression between the Principal Industrial Economies', *Economic Modelling*, 17, 4 December 2000, pp. 515–44; and the monetary union simulation in J. Foreman-Peck, A. Hughes Hallet and Y. Ma, 'European Monetary Union in the Great Depression; a Counterfactual', in D. Currie, and J.D. Whitley (eds), *EMU after Maastricht: Transition or Revaluation?*, London: Lothian Foundation Press, 1995.
25. *Financial Times*, leader 22 May 2003.
26. HM Treasury *Introduction*, paras 46–53. The exercise was conducted on the National Institute for Economic and Social Research's NiGEM model, described in Annex A of the Treasury study and in more detail in the EMU study, *Modelling the transition to EMU* (www.hm-treasury.gov.uk).
27. P. De Grauwe, *Economics of Monetary Union*, Oxford: Oxford University Press, 2000, p. 213.
28. J. Foreman-Peck, *A History of the World Economy: International Economic Relations since 1850*, New York: Harvester Wheatsheaf, 1995, pp. 80–1.

29. D. Roseveare, W. Leibfritz, D. Fore and E. Wurzel, 'Ageing populations, pension systems and government budgets: simulations for 20 OECD countries', *OECD Economics Department Working Paper*, 168, OECD, 1996.

30. J. von Hagen and M. Bruckner, 'Monetary and Fiscal Policy in the European Monetary Union', *Monetary and Economic Studies*, 20, Special Edition, December 2002, pp. 123–54.

31. O. Blanchard and F. Giavazzi, 'Britain misses its euro connection', *Financial Times*, 22 May 2003.

32. The entire evolution of the European Community can be understood as a re-assertion of the nation states involved. A.S. Milward, *The European Rescue of the Nation-State*, London: Routledge, 1992.

33. E.L. Jones, *The European Miracle*, Cambridge: Cambridge University Press, 1981.

34. The classic example is Columbus's progress round the courts of Europe looking for support for his transatlantic voyage but there are many others.

35. To see how the argument works consider a wage-flexible (home) country 1) in, and 2) out, of a wage-inflexible monetary union, when both are subject to an adverse demand shock. Home demand for foreign goods declines by little; because downward wage flexibility maintains the home economy's level of employment and real income. 1) But recessionary pressures from the demand shock spill over from the rest of the monetary union because foreign demand for exports falls, under what is in effect a fixed exchange rate. The flexible home country holds up others' income but suffers from rigid foreigners' falling income under the (permanently) fixed exchange rate. 2) Outside the union, with a floating exchange rate, greater unemployment in the foreign country would be associated with a depreciating (foreign) exchange rate (because of lower imports and interest rates) that would encourage foreigners' export sales and import substitution. This accelerates recovery from the negative demand shock, and so ultimately more quickly restores the demand for the home country's exports.

36. A. Hughes Hallett, 'Britain and the Euro', *Atlantic Economic Journal*, 30, 2002, pp. 335–48.

8

The EMU in a European Perspective: Lessons from Monetary Regimes in the Twentieth Century

Jonas Ljungberg

Exchange rate economics is surrounded by mystery. For example, in a recent article in the Stockholm daily *Dagens Nyheter* (19 April 2003), four former and present chairmen of the board of the Bank of Sweden, the most well-known of which was the former finance minister Feldt, came up with the following propositions:

1. Sweden has benefited from a fixed exchange rate during 'most of the 20th century'.
2. 'Large parts of Europe' have benefited from fixed exchange rates during the last two decades.
3. As a testimony to that Denmark, with fixed exchange rate, is compared with floating Sweden: during the last two decades the living standard of the average Danish household has overtaken and forged ahead of the average Swedish household.

Needless to say, Feldt and associates were lining up with a euro 'Yes' in the Swedish referendum which will give Sweden not only an 'irrevocably' fixed exchange rate with the other euro countries but also a common currency.

However, it is worth scrutinizing these propositions somewhat; they are a bit careless with both facts and causality. Starting with the last proposition, it is wishful thinking that Swedes would have been richer if the Swedish krona had upheld its exchange rate against the Danish krona. It is true that since 1980 the Swedish krona has lost almost 40 per cent of its value compared to the Danish[1] and this is, of course, a source of distress for Swedes visiting Copenhagen. According to Feldt and associates the Swedish average household lost 23 per cent of its purchasing power relative to the Danish. This loss would, however, have been even bigger if the Swedish krona had not depreciated. An economy that does not keep pace with the productivity change among its partners abroad has two alternatives, or a mix of both: either to let the currency depreciate, thereby making exports cheaper and imports more expensive, or to defend the exchange rate by a deflationary policy that brings down prices and costs. 'Costs' primarily means wages and salaries, which is why the alternative to depreciation, the deflationary policy, implies cuts in earnings. Failure, under the fixed exchange rate, to pursue such a deflationary policy will instead result in higher unemployment which is the reality of most euro countries today. In conclusion, the 40 per cent loss of value of the Swedish krona relative to the Danish is not a cause of the relative decrease of Swedish welfare. On the contrary, the fall of the currency actually mitigated the decrease of the Swedish living standard.

There is a second line of the argument, saying that the currency depreciation softens competition and therefore makes firms less apt to improve productivity. Certainly there is some truth in this but there are also other factors at work that may, as will be shown in a while, offset this effect.

This leads to the second proposition, that 'large parts of Europe', that is, the EU, have for two decades had fixed exchange rates. The proposition does not square well with the exchange rate movements among the European currencies in the 1980s and 1990s. Between 1980 and 1995, for example, the Italian lira decreased 59 per cent against the German mark, the British pound decreased 47 per cent, the French franc 33 per cent and the Danish krona 21 per cent. It should be noted that a greater part of these changes took place during the 1980s, thus before the EMS crisis of 1992–3 (to which I will return below).

Furthermore, it should be noted that when Feldt and associates describe this period as a period of fixed exchange rates they follow a popular but nonetheless unenlightened tradition in Swedish public discourse. According to this tradition Sweden has repeatedly taken recourse to devaluations whereas other countries have not. However, the difference is only one of degree, and of vocabulary. Within the

European Exchange Rate Mechanism, in which Sweden did not take part except as a volunteer in 1991-2, the concepts 'devaluation' and 'revaluation' were substituted by the Orwellian 'realignment'.

Concomitantly with the fall of the lira, the pound, the franc and the Danish krona relative to the German mark, the economic growth of these countries was faster than for Germany. Over the period 1980-95, the GDP per capita rose relative to that of Germany – by a petty 1 per cent in France, yet by significant 8 per cent in Italy and 11 and 12 per cent in Britain and Denmark, respectively.[2] The development is more easily seen in Figures 8.1–8.5. Obviously, contrary to the belief of Feldt and associates, if there is any correlation in recent European economic history between a strong currency and economic growth it is a negative correlation. Should one make a generalization from these five cases of the 1980s and 1990s, it must be that a weak currency does not necessarily imply faster growth but a strong currency does imply a slower growth. This proposition is also underpinned by the Swiss experience: the Swiss franc has been even harder than the German mark, and the growth of GDP per capita has, for half a century, been slower in Switzerland than in any other Western European country.

One might surmise that the comparisons are spurious due to the peculiar German development. However, the pattern is roughly the same even if we use other countries as numeraire in the cross-country comparisons. Among the 30 possible comparisons three exceptions could be observed. Thus, when comparisons are made with Italy we find that Denmark and Britain have, during shorter periods, improved both currency and income relative to Italy, and when comparisons are made with Sweden, Denmark has persistently improved both currency and income. On this latter, exceptional case Feldt and associates have based their argument and, moreover, drawn illogical inferences about causality. The inference is illogical since correlation is not necessarily causation and, in particular, simple correlation does not reveal the direction of causality.

In this, rather lengthy, introduction I have discussed the second and third propositions of Feldt and associates. In the following sections I will also scrutinize their first proposition that Sweden has benefited from a fixed exchange rate during 'most of the 20th century'. As a case in point, Feldt and associates highlight the Swedish growth performance during the 1960s. However, it is relevant to remember that

Figure 8.1 Exchange rate and real GDP per capita: Denmark compared with Germany

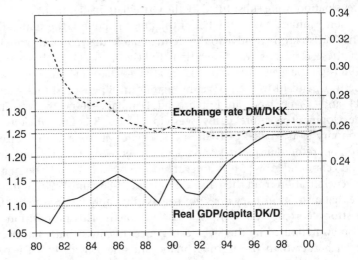

Figure 8.2 Exchange rate and real GDP per capita: France compared with Germany

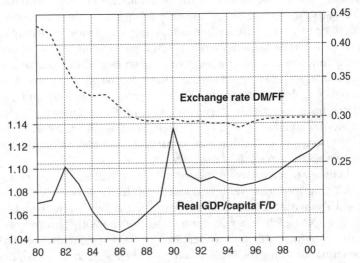

Figure 8.3 Exchange rate and real GDP per capita: Italy compared with Germany

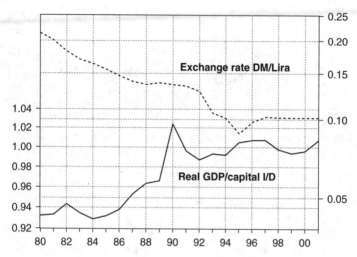

Figure 8.4 Exchange rate and real GDP per capita: Britain compared with Germany

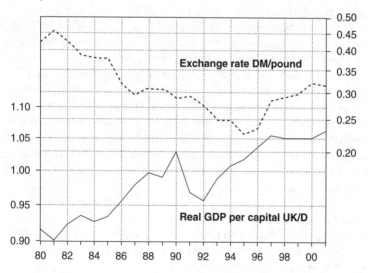

Figure 8.5 Exchange rate and real GDP per capita: Sweden compared with Germany

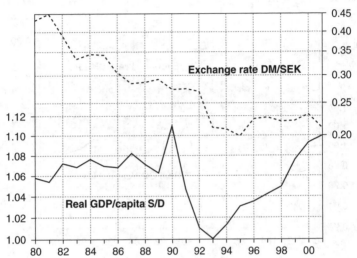

Sources (Figs 8.1–8.5): Monthly exchange rate statistics since 1980 at www.riksbanken.se; Maddison, *The World Economy*; and Groningen Growth and Development Centre and The Conference Board, Total Economy Database, July 2003 (http://www.ggdc.net).

much was different in the 1960s, for example, the overall high growth rates in the period before 1975. Relatively speaking, Sweden had began to lag behind already in the post-war period. In the golden years between 1960 and 1969 only Britain among the present EU countries[3] had a lower GDP per capita growth than Sweden, and the then poor and low-performing Finland and Ireland kept pace with Sweden.

Taking a longer and European, or even global, perspective on fixed exchange rates during the 20th century, it is necessary to sort out different factors. Here, I think it is useful to apply the *open economy trilemma*, also called the *globalization trilemma*. The trilemma points out the impossibility of an economy combining more than two of the following conditions:

- a fixed exchange rate;
- an open capital market, that is, having no restrictions on the capital account in the balance of payments; and
- an independent monetary policy.

The relation between these three conditions is that the exchange rate will vary when capital moves in and out of the country, the value of the currency rising when capital moves in and falling when capital moves out. To defend a fixed exchange rate, the monetary policy must therefore respond to capital movements and has to be given up as an independent instrument of economic policy. An independent instrument means that the interest rate can be chosen with consideration, for example, of unemployment or inflation. Even if the exchange rate is related to the inflation rate, there is a divide between countries that are 'targetting the exchange rate' in their economic policy, for example Denmark today, and countries 'targetting the inflation rate', like Britain and Sweden.

Since the euro actually is floating against the other main currencies of the world, the dollar, the yen and the pound, the European Central Bank (ECB) still has freedom to use monetary policy. However, that is little of a consolation for the different euro countries, since, as is well known, 'one size fits all' is not appropriate for countries with different levels of unemployment and inflation rates. Nevertheless, the open economy trilemma provides a useful lens for a look at monetary regimes.

In a global perspective, including most of the countries in the world, there were three periods of fixed exchange rates in the 20th century. In the next section I will discuss the two earlier periods with the gold standard, and the third section will be devoted to the post-war Bretton Woods system that ended in 1973. The fourth section will discuss the performance of the monetary regimes since then. Focus is on the EMS crisis in 1992–3 and the differences in economic growth within Western Europe thereafter. Section five concludes with an assessment about the three propositions by Feldt and associates, and it draws attention to some similarities between the failed inter-war gold standard and the EMU.

The gold standard

In the last quarter of the 19th century, more and more countries adopted the gold standard that had been pioneered by Britain. The meaning of the gold standard was that a given currency was defined in terms of gold and therefore fixed in its exchange rate towards other currencies. Another characteristic was that gold, and currencies, could move freely between countries. Traditionally it was believed that thereby the gold standard was a self-regulating mechanism, automatically balancing the international economy. Countries with a deficit in foreign trade had to raise the interest rate to attract foreign capital, thus deflating the economy, lowering prices and regaining competitiveness and balance in foreign affairs. Countries with a surplus should allow the surplus to circulate in the economy, induce inflation, lose competitiveness and in that way finally balance its foreign affairs.

Later research has, however, pointed out that during the recurrent banking and financial crises the gold standard was rescued through co-operation between the central banks of the great European powers.[4] The classical gold standard before 1914 can thus be said to have institutionalized a *lender of last resort* function. A lender of last resort can guarantee the liquidity of the economy in times of crisis when otherwise banks would collapse and the economy fall into deflation.

With respect to the open economy trilemma, countries that adhered to the classical gold standard waived the independent monetary policy. Before 1914 democracy and the labour movement still were weak flowers and it was relatively easy for central bankers to ignore the situation in the labour market. The general public probably did not think in terms of economic policy either during that era of globalization, in particular since economic growth was fast and living standards ameliorating.

The gold standard became a victim of World War I. It was reconstructed in the 1920s, though with very different experiences. Inflation had been high during and shortly after the World War and consequently price levels had elevated. The ruling circles of some countries, for example Britain and Sweden, thought that the gold standard should be reconstructed with the pre-war price levels and the pre-war gold parity, that is, with the old exchange rates. To attain that aim the Bank of Sweden sold bonds and drained the circulating money stock in the economy. The deflation was successful, the wholesale prices were halved in a few years, the old parity re-established in 1922 and Sweden was the first country officially to return to the gold standard on 1 April 1924. However, costs were substantial with more than a quarter of the unionized workers unemployed in 1922 and a banking crisis following suit in 1923. Britain also had tough deflation, before attaining gold parity in 1925, and throughout the 1920s she suffered from an overvalued pound, accompanied by stagnating economic growth, persistent unemployment and social unrest.

There were other countries that did not deflate, at least not in the early 1920s. France re-established a fixed exchange rate and the attachment of the franc to gold at a fifth of its pre-war value. That was equal with a 80 per cent tax on assets and sharply reduced the government's domestic war debt. The French economy, however, got back onto its feet and was able even to employ immigrants during the 1920s. Germany is the most known, but not the only, exorbitant case. The domestic war debt, 154 billion marks, equal to about three years' national income, was vaporized through the hyper-inflation and actually converted to the value of a 15 pfennig stamp in the autumn 1923. One year later, in autumn 1924, Germany re-entered the gold standard but seems still today to suffer from the scars of the hyper-inflation. At least, that is the common explanation for her long sustained hard currency policy which was transmitted to the European Central Bank.

Today there is a surprising consensus that the gold standard seriously aggravated the Depression of the 1930s. It is surprising since when Milton Friedman and Anna Schwartz suggested, in 1963,[5] that monetary factors caused the Great Depression they stirred a debate that lasted for more than two decades. It is the more surprising since one of the Keynesians who most ardently had denied the importance of the monetary factors, Peter Temin, in 1989 came up with a synthesis that reconciled elements from both sides.[6]

Whereas Friedman blamed the Depression on deflationary monetary policy in the United States, and meant that it was transmitted to other countries by the fixed exchange rates of the gold standard, Temin derived the whole origin to the *asymmetry* of the gold standard. Today there is much talk about *asymmetrical shocks*, therefore, to avoid confusion, Temin's use of the term 'asymmetry' could be replaced with *double deflationary pressure*. In short, that meant that both deficit countries and surplus countries of the inter-war gold standard pursued a deflationary policy. That is, France and the United States ran a surplus in their foreign trade but instead of pouring the surplus into monetary circulation, according to the so-called rules of the game, the Bank of France and the US Federal Reserve *sterilized* the gold and currencies and piled up huge reserves. The smooth co-operation between central banks from the decades before 1914 had also gone, and as a consequence all countries ran a deflationary policy that steered the world into depression.

Banking and financial crisis in Europe dissipated the gold standard in 1931. Britain and the Nordic countries left the connection with gold and let their currencies float, resulting in depreciation. Figure 8.6 highlights the fact that those who left gold recovered more rapidly from the Depression with a GDP per capita in 1935 well above the level of 1929. Among those who stuck to gold and defended the exchange rate, whether within the Gold Bloc with open capital markets, or whether with currency exchange controls like Germany, Austria and, from 1934, Italy, performed worse. Only Italy was above the level of 1929.

According to one view, countries who devalued the currency exported their problems to those who kept with the gold standard, and that would explain the pattern in Figure 8.6. However, authors like Friedman and Eichengreen do not share that belief and point out that the main aspect was the break with the deflationary constraints, the 'golden fetters'. As a matter of fact, it was the domestic market

Figure 8.6   Percentage change in GDP per capita 1929–35 in countries with different monetary regimes

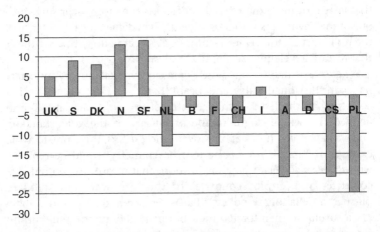

Source: Maddison, *Monitoring the World Economy*; the five from the left abandoned gold in 1931; the next four were the backbone of the Gold Bloc which also included eastern countries, such as Czeckoslovakia and Poland (far right); Italy was on gold until 1934, when exchange controls were introduced and the fixed exchange rate maintained, after the model of Germany and Austria.

and not exports that led Britain and Sweden out of the Depression. Due to the deflation and the dissipation of the gold standard, international economic relations broke down. International trade sharply declined due to the Depression and the concomitant rise of protectionism.

Before 1914, the gold standard worked but in the inter-war period it caused, or at least seriously aggravated, the Depression. With fixed exchange rates and open capital markets, monetary policy should be determined by the rules of the game, according to the open economy trilemma. France and the US, however, chose an independent line and produced double deflationary pressure. The co-operation between central banks, which in the late 19th century had instituted an international lender of last resort, was in the inter-war years replaced by distrust.

The Brettons Woods system

The lessons of the Great Depression were manifest in the international economic regime that emerged after World War II. At its base was the Bretton Woods agreement of 1944 that defined the monetary regime. Exchange rates were fixed but adjustable, allowing a country with recurrent deficits or surpluses to devalue or revalue. The aim was to re-establish the convertibility of the national currencies as quickly as possible, that is, to release the current account in the balance of payments. The Bretton Woods agreement did not, however, judge financial capital movements as beneficial and consequently it continued to restrict the capital account in the balance of payments. With regulated capital markets, the third condition of the open economy trilemma could be left rather unconstrained. Thus, national independence in monetary policy was a feature of the Bretton Woods period.

Another feature of the Bretton Woods system was the creation of the World Bank and the International Monetary Fund (IMF). The informal lender of last resort that had existed under the classical gold standard, but not during its inter-war years, was now given a formal organization. The IMF should also give consent to adjustments, in the form of devaluations and revaluations, of the national currencies but it was often side-stepped.

By providing for liquidity in the international economy Bretton Woods probably prevented a post-war depression. The impact of

Bretton Woods and the post-war battery of international co-operation, the GATT and the Marshall Plan, have been much discussed. Being praised by the first generation of economic historians, who themselves had shared the fears of a post-war depression and took part in the organizational work, the second generation of revisionists diminuated the Bretton Woods system. Now the third generation, emphasizes the importance of the institutions for creating a framework that allowed for the expansion of trade and economic growth.[7]

However, Bretton Woods needed help to get on its feet and get the European currencies convertible against the dollar. The help was supplied by the European Payments Union (EPU), a clearing centre for most of world trade during the years 1950–8. Through the EPU Western Europe could get rid of the bilateral trade characterizing the 1930s and 1940s, and advance multilateral trade. The EPU also took on the role of lender of last resort, for example heading a rescue operation for West Germany in 1950 and for France in 1957.[8]

With convertibility attained in 1958 the EPU could be dissolved and Bretton Woods had its heyday. Despite all arrangements, however, the system was fragile and declined with the weakening of the dollar during the Vietnam War. Finally, it dissipated in 1973 and since then the main currencies have been floating.

The mid-1970s were a turning point in economic development and, as a case in point, the long-term GDP growth rates were generally reduced in the OECD countries and a period of full employment changed to persistent unemployment in Europe. Mentioning the crisis of the 1970s, most people think of oil. Actually a depression hit large sectors of the economy well into the 1980s, some branches such as steel and shipbuilding suffered the most. Whereas there is a broad consensus about the depression of the 1930s, opinion differs about the 1970s.

There is one important aspect that must not be forgotten in the evaluation of the Bretton Woods international economic regime. By contrast with the 1930s, international economic relations did not break down despite the dissipation of the monetary regime. There were some currents of protectionism but international trade was in the main not impeded. Moreover, even if the fixed exchange rates, and the connection between the dollar and gold, were gone, the Bretton Woods organizations, the World Bank and the IMF, remained. A fundamental difference was that inflation accelerated in the 1970s, whereas deflation was the characteristic of the 1930s. Economists were puzzled by this phenomenon, inflation and rising unemployment at the same time, and labelled it *stagflation*. Milton Friedman had an explanation for that, tentatively suggested before the phenomenon appeared, pointing out monetary policy as the cause. What makes Friedman's explanation somewhat narrow is that the issue is confined within a model of a closed economy.[9]

For an explanation of stagflation, it seems more reasonable to look at the international economy; a crucial factor was the behaviour of the oil-exporting countries. Due to the fourfold increase of oil prices in 1973–4 they got huge surpluses but in contrast to France and the US around 1930, the oil-exporting countries did not sterilize the money. The huge amounts of 'petrodollars' were recirculated into the international economy which was caught with inflation. Had the oil-exporting countries behaved like France and the US around 1930, and stored the money, the world would probably have suffered from deflation in the 1970s. The consequences would have been even worse than what actually became the case.

The European Monetary System and the Monetary Union

After the breakdown of the Bretton Woods system in 1973, the international economic regime has been largely reformed and the conditions of the open economy trilemma turned around. First, exchange rates have become globally floating, even if regional arrangements have been frequent. Thus, most Western European currencies were anchored to the German mark, in the 1970s within the 'Snake' and from 1979 within the European Monetary System (EMS). Second, instead of control on national capital accounts, capital movements have been liberalized which means that there is today a radically greater capital market than in the post-war decades. With these two conditions changing place, there is still room for an independent monetary policy, if the institutional instrument of a central bank is there. However, within the EMS, as well as within its successor the Economic and Monetary Union (EMU), that 'independence' became orchestrated by the German *Bundesbank* and then by the European Central Bank (ECB).

The fixed arrangement of the 'Snake' and the EMS was of a peculiar sort that allowed repeated devaluations against the German mark.

First there was a band of variability, giving room for movements of 2.25 per cent (6 per cent for Italy), in both directions of the exchange rate.[10] Since inflation rates diverged between the participating countries that variability was inadequate without most countries being forced to pursue a radical deflationary policy. To avoid this, eleven collective devaluations, called 'realignments', were undertaken from the launch of the EMS in March 1979 to January 1987.[11] Yet, from 1987 onward it became a true system of fixed exchange rates.

The late 1980s saw an acceleration of economic growth in most countries and generally inflation was dampened, as tension on the exchange rates had eased. It was also in this climate that the construction of the EMU was drafted and laid down in the Treaty of Maastricht, first negotiated in December 1991. It did not last long, however. A recession began in 1990 and, combined with a bubble in real estate values, a financial crisis was in ferment. The German reunification in October 1990 as well as the dissolution of the Soviet Union in the following year were two shocks that further contributed to the instability. Despite a fall in GDP of the unified Germany in 1990, the favourable exchange of German marks for East marks and other adaptations in the East created a boom in demand that exerted an inflationary pressure on the price level. Inflation was, though, customarily controlled by interest rate increases by the *Bundesbank*.

Other countries within the EMS in this situation needed an even lower inflation rate than Germany and, before the crisis had fully evolved, urged the Germans to lower interest rates. Germany refused and the alternative for the other EMS countries, to devalue, was still, in early September 1992, not acceptable since fixed exchange rates were, according to the Maastricht Treaty, the road to the single currency.[12] After Finland, yet not a member of the EU or the EMS, had left the peg of the markka to the ecu (European Currency Unit, forerunner of the euro) on 8 September 1992, the EMS crisis evolved rapidly. Despite the fact that the lira, the pound, the Spanish peseta and the Portuguese escudo had been severely strained for months, even the week before Finland uncorked the crisis the IMF – supervisor of the international economy – had not seen any signs in the stars.[13]

It is a remarkable fact that the crisis was so unexpected. The early 1990s were turbulent and Finland had already devalued once, in December 1991, while keeping the connection between the markka and the ecu. Finland was in a severe recession due to the loss of its export market in the Soviet Union. Moreover, German reunification, given the monetary policy of the *Bundesbank* and the rigid exchange rates, also put a strain on European economies. Furthermore, real estate values (for example, London Docklands), were in free fall after having lured investors with soaring prices for some years. Nevertheless, the leading architects of the EMU, as contained in the Maastricht Treaty, were full of confidence about the future: 'Overall there is therefore little reason to believe that the EMS would be destabilized by random self-fulfilling attacks in the early 1990s. There is therefore no need to construct special safeguards against turbulences in financial markets.'[14]

Pegged (in a rather ill-timed move) to the ecu in May 1991, but like the Finnish markka not a member of the EMS, the Swedish krona was among the first being attacked in September 1992, together with the pound and the lira. Britain and Italy dropped the peg and let their currencies float. Swedish Prime Minister Carl Bildt declared, however, that there was only 'one single course', and that was the necessity of endurance and not to touch the peg. Financial markets saw through him, of course, and not even an interest rate of 500 per cent could save the krona. According to the Bank of International Settlements, reserves amounting to US $26 billion poured out of Sweden in the week before the abandonement of the peg on 19 November.[15] The amount was equal to 12 per cent of Sweden's GDP.

The EMS crisis rolled on into 1993. Ireland, who together with Spain and Portugal had tightened capital controls in the preceding year, now abolished them in January and instead devalued the punt by 10 per cent. For other countries, rapid capital movements continued to exert pressure on the exchange rates and the hope was that the *Bundesbank* would cut the German interest rate. Eventually, in July, an agreement was reached to drop the fixed exchange rates. Formally, the Exchange Rate Mechanism within the EMS was maintained but the band width was increased from 4.5 per cent (−2.25 to +2.25) to 30 per cent. Tensions eased and the windy financial markets calmed down. There is still no consensus view on the EMS crisis, whether economies were sound and a victim of self-fulfilling attacks of speculators or whether real economic weakness rendered them open to attacks. The bottom line remains, however, that without fixed exchange rates from 1987 no targets for the attacks had existed and adaptations to the new circumstances were much smoother.

Next to Finland, Sweden fell deepest in the recession and, in the three years 1991–3, lost more than 6 per cent of its GDP per capita. Most of the Finnish decrease came, however, in 1991 following the Soviet collapse and the regress in 1992–3 was roughly the same in both these Nordic countries. It is clear that the pegging of the krona in 1991 in a fixed exchange rate with the ecu was very unfortunate and significantly contributed to the Swedish deterioration in the OECD income leaugue. Yet, the EMS crisis hurt all of Western Europe. Of 14 present members in the EU[16] only Ireland, the Netherlands and Denmark did *not* have negative economic growth in 1993. It thus seems as if the proposition by Feldt and associates, that 'large parts of Europe' have benefited from fixed exchange rates during the last two decades is particularly ill-founded.

When the EMS crisis evolved it was perceived as a test of the commitment of governments to proceed with the Maastricht Treaty to monetary union. The outcome raised doubts about the viability of the whole project but favourable economic conditions during the latter part of the 1990s made it possible to launch the euro. Yet, the period after 1993 has seen two opposite monetary policies within the EU. One became targeting the exchange rate, followed by the 'irrevocably' fixed exchange rate within the eurozone with Denmark as associate. The other became targeting the inflation, as in Britain and Sweden. It could be argued that the eurozone is also targeting inflation now but that this is being done through the 'one size fits all policy' of the ECB. According to the open economy trilemma the difference remains between floating Britain and Sweden, and the eurozone and Denmark with fixed exchange rates. The former have room for an independent monetary policy which the latter have not.

Now, the growth performance of the different countries may show whether 'large parts of Europe' have benefited from fixed exchange rates in the period after the EMS crisis. Table 8.1 shows the economic growth of the present EU members, minus Luxembourg but including Norway and Switzerland, 1994–2002. For comparison the Bretton Woods period, 1950–73, and the post-Bretton Woods period up to 1993 are included. During the recent decade some countries of the eurozone have performed very well, better than Britain and Sweden. However, it is interesting to note that none of those countries that were wealthier than Sweden in 1993 have grown faster since then. Similarly, during the last decade Britain has caught up with all countries that

Table 8.1 Annual percentage change in GDP per capita 1950–2002, and GDP per capita levels in 1993

Country ranked according to growth 1994–2002	GDP per capita in 1993 (1990 PPP dollars)	Annual change 1950–73	Annual change 1974–93	Annual change 1994–2002
Ireland	12567	3.0	2.9	7.5
Finland	14873	4.0	2.1	3.7
Spain	12352	5.5	1.8	3.3
Greece	9982	6.0	1.5	3.2
Portugal	11194	5.4	2.7	3.2
Sweden	16556	3.2	1.3	2.9
Netherlands	17747	3.4	1.5	2.6
United Kingdom	16369	2.3	2.0	2.3
Belgium	17354	3.4	1.8	2.2
Austria	17201	4.7	2.1	2.1
Denmark	18945	3.3	1.9	2.0
France	18060	4.0	1.7	2.0
Italy	16430	4.9	2.4	1.7
Germany	16544	4.6	1.8	1.5
Outside EU:				
Norway	19873	3.1	2.7	2.5
Switzerland	20724	3.0	1.1	1.3

Source: Maddison, *The World Economy*. The period 1994–2002 is computed from series available at Groningen Growth and Development Centre and the Conference Board, Total Economy Database, July 2003 (http://www.ggdc.net).

were wealthier than it was in 1993, except Sweden and the Netherlands. One can conclude that the usual complaints in the Swedish public debate that Sweden is lagging behind the rest of Europe are outdated.

Sweden's economic growth was inferior to the rest of Western Europe, except Switzerland, from the breakdown of the Bretton Woods system through the EMS crisis. By contrast with the period after 1973, the 1950s and 1960s are often praised as the 'golden age' of high growth rates. It should not be forgotten, however, that almost all countries in Western Europe also had a higher growth than Sweden in the period 1950–73.

Could it then be concluded that the Swedish recovery after 1993 is due to the monetary policy and the floating krona? It has probably contributed but the recent high growth should be seen against the slowdown in the preceding two decades. The Swedish economy was characterized by heavy industries and large firms that were severely hit by the structural crisis in the mid-1970s. Shipbuilding and steel, along with most of textiles, were nationalized before 1980, by a centre-liberal government, and heavily subsidized. However, similar policies were commonplace all over Europe, supported by the European Commisson and, paradoxically, increased during Margaret Thatcher's premiership in Britain.[17]

Swedish shipbuilding, having been second only to Japan as regards launched tonnage and leading in productivity, was closed down in the mid-1980s. Steel was trimmed but profitable again in 1985. New computer technology was, however, at the core of the transformation of Swedish business. That is mirrored by the very high investments in research and development, and by a very large consumption of IT equipment. The transformation from a structure, inherited since the 'Second Industrial Revolution' of the early 20th century, to the new structure of the 'Third Industrial Revolution', was probably more thorough-going than in most other countries. When the old was destructed and the new created, productivity could but fall, and Sweden but lag behind.

The recent growth recovery could thus largely be seen as an explanation to Solow's *productivity paradox*. Robert Solow, honoured with the Nobel Memorial Prize for his contributions to the theory of economic growth, remarked in 1987: 'You can see the computer age everywhere but in the productivity statistics.'[18] Recent research has uncovered that the first signs of the positive impact of introduction of a new technology, such as computers or electricity, take some time to become apparent. Swedish development is a case in point.[19] Economic policy is important but it is easy to overestimate its role. It sets the conditions for the working of the economy but there are also other conditions, laid down in traditions and structures that are part of a country's history. Such factors fundamentally determine economic growth and they cannot simply be substituted by another economic policy. On the other hand, poor economic policy can have disastrous effects, as the EMS crisis testifies.

Conclusion

The only periods of the 20th century when Europe, and Sweden, might have benefited from fixed exchange rates were before 1914 and 1950–73. Both periods succeeded, however, due to peculiar, and scarcely desirable or possible, combinations of the open economy trilemma. The classical gold standard did not have much room for modern democracy and welfare policy. The Bretton Woods regime had little room for free capital movements. Over the last decade, when Sweden has pursued a consequent float, her economic performance has, relatively speaking, been better than ever since 1950. During the Bretton Woods period Swedish economic growth was clearly *below* the Western European average, whereas it has been *above* the average since 1993. The improvement is certainly not caused by good monetary policy but it could well have been aborted by a bad monetary policy.

What is distressing is that the EMU is a burden for Europe. It might be that the 'single currency' can contain speculative attacks of the sort that evolved during the EMS crisis. However, overvaluation of currencies that were part of the EMS crisis will still reappear as real economic tensions in the form of regional unemployment and inflation.

When the international economic regime was designed for the post-war period, lessons were drawn from the 1930s. Deflation and unemployment were seen as the great fear. In the ongoing reform of the economic regime, lessons are one-sidedly drawn from the 1970s and 1980s. Inflation has become the overwhelming fear. That is understandable, however, when combined with the belief that we now face *The End of History*, it implies a big risk.[20] The EMU is designed as if there are no big structural changes or unexpected events ahead, since its constitutional arrangements are only designed for defence against the fear of the 1970s and 1980s, namely inflation.

Compared with earlier monetary regimes, the EMU has most similarities with the inter-war gold standard. The double deflationary pressure of the inter-war gold standard resurfaces in the single focus on anti-inflation policy of the EMU. The failure to bring up a lender of last resort during the Depression of the 1930s is, contrary to any other truly international monetary regime of the 20th century, formally instituted in the EMU, for example, through the so-called 'no-bail-out clause'.[21] Thus, the decapitated national central banks are prohibited from giving credit support to each other, and there is the famous (or, infamous) prescription of penalties for countries that suffer fiscal deficits. Given the history of the late 1970s and 1980s, when even Margaret Thatcher poured billions of pounds into ailing steel mills and coal mines, there are arguments for a policy that can moderate public expenditures. However, it is scarcely wise to make a policy irrevocable. On the eve of the EMS crisis the architects of the EMU could not even imagine a need for 'safeguards' against financial and banking crises. Yet, today, with persistent unemployment in the core countries, with the eastern enlargement, with increasing demands on public welfare due to ageing populations, it should be easy to see that the way ahead is not evenly paved. Unfortunately, the EMU prescribes that these problems must be fought with one arm tied behind the back.

Notes

1. All data on exchange rates are based on the monthly statistics published at the web site of the Bank of Sweden, www.riksbanken.se
2. Based on A. Maddison, *The World Economy: A Millennial Perspective*, Paris: OECD, 2001; GDP/capita for 'Germany' includes both East and West. The growth rate for West Germany was slightly higher but would only change the position relative to France. The level of GDP per capita was 9 per cent higher in West Germany than the average for all Germany both in 1980 and in 1989. A. Maddison, *Monitoring the World Economy, 1820–1992*, Paris: OECD, 1995.
3. Except Luxembourg, for which data are missing in the works by Maddison, referred to in note 2; Swedish growth was also higher than for Germany when the East is included.
4. See, for example, B. Eichengreen, *Golden Fetters: The Gold Standard and the Great Depression, 1919–1939*, Oxford: Oxford University Press, 1992; and B. Eichengreen, *Globalizing Capital: A History of the International Monetary System*, Princeton, NJ: Princeton University Press, 1996.
5. M. Friedman and A.J. Schwartz, *The Monetary History of the United States, 1867–1960*, Princeton, NJ: Princeton University Press, 1963.
6. P. Temin, *Lessons from the Great Depression*, Cambridge, Mass.: MIT Press, 1989. Though Temin, in his previous book, *Did Monetary Forces Cause the Great Depression* (New York: Norton, 1976), was a traditional Keynesian, in 1989 he managed to derive his new position from a text by Keynes, forgotten by the master's disciples. With modern terminology and according to Temin, Keynes had once highlighted monetary policy as the *exogenous shock* that set off the recession but then became occupied with the *propagating mechanism*, of insufficient demand and investments, that rolled on the Depression.
7. For example, B. Eichengreen (ed.), *Europe's Post-War Recovery*, Cambridge: Cambridge University Press, 1994; and L. Schön, *En modern svensk ekonomisk historia. Tillväxt och omvandling under två sekel*, Stockholm: SNS, 2000.
8. See J. Kaplan and G. Schleiminger, *The European Payments Union: Financial Diplomacy in the 1950s*, Oxford: Clarendon Press, 1989.

9. M. Friedman, 'The Role of Monetary Policy', *American Economic Review*, 58 (1), 1968, pp. 1–17. However, the actual concept of stagflation is not to be found here, or the 'vertical Phillips curve' which is also explained.
10. P. De Grauwe, *Economics of Monetary Union*, Oxford: Oxford University Press, 2000, p. 98. Also Spain, joining EMS in 1989, Britain, joining in 1990, and Portugal, joining in April 1992 (!) had the 6 + 6 per cent band width.
11. D. Gros and N. Thygesen, *European Monetary Integration. From the European Monetary System to the European Monetary Union*, London: Longman, 1992, p. 68.
12. Negotiations at Bath, first week in September 1992. For an account of events and explanations, see B. Eichengreen, *Capital Flows and Crises*, Cambridge, Mass.: MIT Press, 2003, chapter 8. Striking, though, is Eichengreen's narrow focus that largely ignores the concomitant real estate bubble and banking crises in several countries.
13. *Ibid.*, p. 229.
14. Gros and Thygesen, *European Monetary Integration*, p. 166. Foreword dated in March 1992.
15. Eichengreen, *Capital Flows*, p. 220; also in Eichengreen, *Globalizing Capital*, p. 174.
16. Not including Luxembourg.
17. See Y. Mény and V. Wright (eds), *The Politics of Steel: Western Europe and the Steel Industry in the Crisis Years (1974–1984)*, Berlin: W. de Gruyter, 1986; and G.F. Dudley and J.J. Richardson, *Politics and Steel in Britain. The Life and Time of the British Steel Corporation*, Aldershot: Dartmouth, 1990. Articles in *The Economist* provide evidence of substantial state support to steel in Germany, France and Italy at least well into the 1990s (references in J. Ljungberg, 'Kol och stål – starka "särintressen" i Västeuropa', *Historisk tidskrift*, 2, 1995, pp. 243–52).
18. Quoted from N. Crafts, 'The Solow Productivity Paradox in Historical Perspective', *CEPR Discussion Paper 3142*, 2001.
19. Schön, *En modern svensk ekonomisk historia*, pp. 509f.
20. Cf. F. Fukuyama, *The End of History and the Last Man*, New York: Free Press, 1992.
21. Article 104 in the original Maastricht Treaty.

9
National Policy in Disguise: A Historical Interpretation of the EMU

Hans Albin Larsson

It is hardly possible to discuss future aspects of the European Union without considering the effects of EMU; nor to form opinions on EMU without first considering what purposes the EU should serve, what it should be, and how it should be governed.

Only three of the present 15 EU member states have decided to refer EMU membership to national referenda. Denmark voted against in 2000; Sweden decided not to in 2003; and the United Kingdom, at the time of publishing, has not yet set the date for any referendum. National referenda, as opposed to parliamentary resolutions, give rise to a wider public debate on the pros and cons of any given proposition. This is true also in the matter of the EMU. Politicians seek confirmation of their viewpoints in science and research. What outcome would best serve Sweden and the United Kingdom, a 'yes' or a 'no'? What would be best for Europe? Answers differ, depending on whether they are provided by scientists, politicians, or representatives of trade and industry, agriculture etc. Some claim to know, but for the most part, subjective interpretations are offered, based on individual values. It is not possible to make any definite predictions of the future, or is it? This is a matter of concern. If Sweden votes for EMU membership, it is not possible to predict if that will have a positive or a negative effect on the economy. There may be more or less firm beliefs; however, whether EMU membership will have a financially positive or negative influence remains an open question. Should higher or lower wages, more or less trade union power, increased or decreased labour market mobility be considered as positive or negative effects? Which of any number of scenarios will occur, and under what circumstances? However, the fact is that key decisive functions will be transferred from the *Sveriges Riksbank* and the Bank of England to the European Central Bank (ECB), should Sweden and the United Kingdom decide to join the EMU. It is indisputable that change will be an unavoidable consequence, but whether this will be positive or negative is an entirely subjective interpretation. Conclusions reached are based on the observer's own values. Thus, the purpose of the following chapter is to discuss European integration theory and, from this approach, as well as a historical perspective, submit an interpretation of political motives behind the EMU.

As part of the negotiations of the Treaty of Nice in 2000, the EU heads of state and government agreed to appoint the European Convention on the future development of the EU. The Convention's proposal, which was submitted in June 2003, is expected to form the basis for decisions to be taken at the 2004 Intergovernmental Conference. Issues to be considered are the future structure of the EU, together with relations and influence of the member states due to the imminent enlargement of the Union. The result of the Treaty of Nice *per se* was an increase in supranational power and a decrease in influence of, in particular, the small countries. One explanation for this was that the enlarged Union would need a simplified decisionmaking process in order to function smoothly.

Following the Treaty of Nice, the number of issues that may be decided by a qualified majority by the Council of Ministers became significantly higher. The right of veto was also abolished in some 40 other areas; however, decisions on fiscal policy and some areas of social policy still require unanimity. From 2005, new regulations will come into effect concerning decisions made by qualified majority.[1] In 2001, the *Riksdag* called attention to the fact that, as a result of the Treaty of Nice, some new, yet limited, decisionmaking authorities have been transferred to the European Community. 'Co-operation was not changed by the Treaty of Nice, but will, in essence, retain is international character.'[2] In what ways, then, will the basis of co-operation be influenced by the EMU? A natural point of departure for an interpretation would be to look more closely at the theoretical arguments which support the integration of the European Union.

EU integration theory

Functionalism, renaissance of the nation state, idealism, exercise of power – or all of these simultaneously?

Is it possible to find motivations for the organizational and decision-making processes of the EU in scientific research? Explanations can be found, however, and some of these border on being motivations of sorts, or legitimations. Whether the increasing centralization of decisionmaking to the EU level will involve development towards federalism, or any other form, is one of the most frequent issues of debate among political scientists as well as politicians. Opinions differ widely on whether EU decisionmaking processes unduly favour certain interests, whether supranationality is too far-reaching, or too limited, and how any possible changes would be made.

One theoretical approach, which developed in the first few years after World War II, is often described as functionalism. According to that approach, the system of sovereign states can or would be replaced by a system of international organizations taking responsibility for regulatory systems of certain common issues or functions, such as transportation, health care, education, technological development etc. British political scientist David Mitrany was of the opinion that it would be more appropriate for specifically designated regional or global organizations to be in charge of such issues, than relinquishing them to nation states. A functional integration would thereby be achieved, which would lead to political power being released by the nation states in favour of a kind of co-ordinated welfare state.[3]

From the American perspective, encouraging this approach to European co-operation was natural, since it contributed to maintaining a strong front against Stalinist Soviet Union. The Cold War was thus a significant factor behind the establishment of the European Coal and Steel Community, and later the Treaty of Rome, and the EEC.[4] The American political scientist Karl Deutsch, as opposed to representatives of functionalist theory, emphasizes this background, pointing to the Western Transatlantic community as an important reason for West-European integration.[5]

In the scholarly debate, the establishment of common institutions is scientifically motivated by the so-called neofunctionalist integration theory, which was first formulated by American political scientists at Stanford University. According to this approach, nation states, by successively releasing competence within defined issue areas to common supranational institutions, will become politically more closely united, and eventually establish a political union. Under the influence of the Cold War and the American political model, they could foresee increasing European integration as both natural and desirable.[6] The neofunctionalist approach was highly normative, and was criticized for not giving due consideration to the functions of nation states, and thereby their importance in the post-war European situation. The French veto in 1963 against UK membership of the EEC was seen as a sign that the new situation of supranational organized co-operation did not basically alter the political behaviour of nation states, but primarily involved the creation of a new arena for nation state politics.[7] More recent research to a larger extent suggests that the nation state remains a fundamental entity. A possible development, which would strengthen the nation state, could then be to find solutions to its problems at the supranational level. Within areas, which are regarded by the nation states themselves as extremely important and of vital national interest, self-determination would be prefered in the future instead of being forced to submission with the ensuing dissent and distrust.[8]

Among the first generation of historians studying European integration there was a pronounced disposition in favour of European unification, which induced them to regard the post-war European movement, arising in certain countries, as the founder of the European Community in the 1950s. However, this interpretation was later rejected by a number of succeeding historians, among them the British economic historian Alan S. Milward. According to Milward and others, the European Community is not the antithesis of the nation state, but another step forward in its long evolution. The Community, handling some common functions, is considered as necessary for the survival of the nation state.[9] Never before, had nation states found more support among their own populations than during the establishment of the modern welfare state which was for the benefit of the entire population. Therefore, the emergence of European co-operation has substantially strengthened the nation state, according to Milward. However, his line of argument is, in essence, based on the period up to 1970. The transference of decisionmaking to the supranational level, and the extensive homogenization of rules and regulations from the end of the 1980s, cannot be assessed in the same way as the 'golden age' of rapid growth, that is the 1950s and 1960s. Milward is fully aware of this, and argues that latter-day state difficulties in controlling finances and collecting taxes may make it more difficult for the nation state to assert itself.[10]

Transnational movement of capital, widespread public utilization of the Internet, international education programmes etc., have sometimes been assumed to reduce the importance of national identity. However, cultural research maintains the opposite, not referring to the nationally newly awakened Eastern Europe, but rather to the West-European EU member states. One representative of this approach is the Dutch social psychologist Geert Hofstede, who maintains that modern technology can only to a limited extent influence national identity. He argues, for example, that the cultural demarcation line, which coincided with the northern frontier of the Roman Empire, is still evident. Since nation states are products of history, they are more deeply rooted in the mind than institutions and external regulatory frameworks. Even though they sometimes can be difficult to trace, they are there and will remain in the foreseeable future, according to Hofstede.[11]

Another type of theory concerning the European future has been suggested by researchers concentrating on co-operation within and between regions. They assume that the abolition of borders and national distinctions in legislation and regulatory frameworks have thoroughly diminished local and regional dependence on national decisionmakers, parliaments and governments. Instead, a great number of networks have emerged, managing their own business within the framework of common European legislation. Such networks may consist of private individuals, companies, local authorities, organizations and regional institutions, or combinations of these. Daily contact creates a climate of decisionmaking, which may be characterized as 'governing without a government'. German political scientist Beate Kohler-Koch maintains that local and regional networks themselves are able to determine appropriate rules and regulations, therefore reducing the need for decisionmaking at a national level. National loyalties and representative democracy then become less important, since such networks are better at solving political problems.[12]

Still another theoretical approach assumes that the toned-down importance of national borders will be replaced by judicial spectra at different levels. According to this view, the future Europe will not be replaced by some kind of federal organization, but the decisionmaking process will revolve around several different dimensions. The American political scientist Philippe C. Schmitter argues that parliamentarism and representative democracy will naturally become less important in the process of ongoing integration. His point of departure is that territories, that is geographical divisions, and permanent or mobile functions of the decisionmaking system, will become more important than people's national identity. The system of nation states will most probably be replaced by a 'condominium' ('commonwealth') within the EU, where both territories and functions will fluctuate according to circumstances and over time. The limits and extent of this will depend on what identity and what political alliances are possible from one time to another. Thus, there are circumstances that recall situations that to a not insignificant degree will be reminiscent of the feudal division of Europe in the Middle Ages, when one and the same area could be part of diverse collection of larger and smaller entities.[13]

Political scientist Kjell Goldmann takes a distinctly idealistic approach, manifest in his recently published study on the EU as an ideological project. On the basis of an assessment of the fundamental principles of conservatism, liberalism, democratic socialism and eco-logism, Goldmann suggests his comparatively modest hypothesis that 'European project dynamism to some extent depends on conservative, liberal, social democratic and ecologistical views having reached the same conclusion on the main issue, that is the European project should be promoted.'[14]

Goldmann is of the opinion that ideological traditions have a special position in the dynamic sphere between supranational and national interests. These are structural; 'they represent a political willpower without being national'.[15] According to Goldmann, the 'European project' is driven by liberal internationalism and moderate conservatism in combination with social democratic and ecological instrumentalism:

> The EU has reached a point where it is seen as a resource to avert threats, which are emphasized to a various extent and in different ways by separate ideological traditions, that is threats against peace, nations, the welfare society and the environment. The sum total of this is a political project of a hue of pale blue, pale red and pale green.[16]

The EU may be interpreted as an ideological project, in which different traditions have influenced each other into a common European supraideology:

> Thus: the European project is propelled by a broad coalition with an optimistic view of institutional change. This coalition shares common ideals about the nation state, peace, solidarity and environmental concerns and, of course, democracy; and finds within the European project an opportunity to reinforce them all. The coalition is attacked from the right and left, yet at present stands firm.[17]

Comment

An immediate reflection on the reviewed theories is that the interpretations of current European and EU development almost without exception, tacitly though implicitly, assume that the European countries are similar, or that their national problems, as related to the EU, are similar. Consequently, it becomes natural for those researchers to seek to generalize problems and solutions. The historically unique in the political life, culture, history and perception of problems of each member state does not to any appreciable extent seem to have influenced the advocates of the interpretations and theories presented above. Thus, both Milward's ideas on the reinforcement of the nation state as well as the American functionalists' views about the logic of joint development may be seen as a result of approaches based on particular circumstances. Milward's reasoning is based on the fact that the high-growth decades led to a strengthening of the then member states at a national level; however, actually other West-European countries, for example the Nordic countries, also experienced a higher degree of self-assuredness than ever before during this period. Milward's hypothesis may be true for some countries under certain circumstances, but it can not be generalized, that is, taken for a correct interpretation of situations in other countries some decades later. Also the view represented by Beate Kohler-Koch, that is that the increasing role of local and regional networks will reduce the importance of the national power, could be seen as true only to a limited extent. Within the EU core area, geographical distances are very short, and within the former Holy Roman Empire there are historical traditions of a decentralized structure, where central decisionmaking was an exception. Moreover, Germany is a federal state and has as, for example, Spain, the prerequisites for the development of a political order such as that analyzed by Kohler-Koch and others, and which they anticipate to be enlarged in the future. Other parts of the EU and Europe, however, have completely different preconditions and other traditions.

Kjell Goldmann's reasoning about different ideological traditions merging into a common European supraideology may be relevant for some of the larger member states, or for their representatives, irrespective of their ideology, and some sympathizers in other, smaller member states, but not from any general point of view. What seems to connect those who support the 'European project', in Goldmann's interpretation, may for the larger member states be the possibility of reaching important ideological goals through supranationality. In the smaller member states, however, it is rare for anyone other than representatives of the establishment to think that the advantages of supranationality outweigh the disadvantages. That is not surprising, as the smaller countries for the most part only have marginal influence over supranational decisions. To conclude, it may be maintained that generalizing interpretations of EU integration, focusing on a certain period of time (for example, the 1960s), certain areas (for example, France, Germany or the Benelux), certain political and social layers (such as some members of the European parliament or some political parties) are only true to a limited extent. History may be interpreted in different ways, and historical and cultural background factors are not always easily discernible when the focus is on current politics. It is hardly possible to disregard the historical differences between Europe's nation states, if it is seriously intended to bring them together into a workable union. Social engineering is always more successful in theory than in practice.

The democratic deficit

The question of how the EU should be governed is, however, always relevant, particularly when the imminent enlargement into Eastern Europe and the proposal of the Convention are taken into account. The reason is that the Union's decisionmaking process is significantly at variance with that of normal democracies, as the decisionmakers cannot be held politically responsible, and decisions largely are taken without public control. The decisionmaking process has emerged successively, although, even in the formation of the Coal and Steel

Community, a swift decisionmaking process was given priority over a democratic one, clearly for reasons of efficiency. Already the Schuman Plan indicated that the Community should not have the character of a state with its own constitution, yet the co-operation was to be supervised by a supranational authority, which also should exercise judicial power in case of disputes between conflicting interests. The purpose of the Plan was to enable immediate action to be taken within a limited but decisive field.[18] Jean Monnet, who was one of its founding fathers, in a classified memo pointed out, on account of the acute situation of the Cold War, the necessity for immediate and concrete action; that action was important to infuse new hope in a situation where the Soviet threat was acutely felt.[19]

The decisionmaking process that emerged in 1950–1 was later established and has developed into the present characteristic feature of the EU. The absence of any possibility of obtaining democratic responsibility is often called the democratic deficit in the current debate. An increasingly debated question, which is also becoming more important following the increasing influence of the Union, is how to respond to this constitutional problem. Political scientist Sverker Gustavsson observes that judicial development is supranational to a greater extent than the demand for democratic responsibility would require. A democratic powerbase is lacking, although the European judicial system has, in a federal manner, direct effect and a supreme position. Gustavsson is of the opinion that the debate on asymmetry is, in part, based on the wrong assumptions. A case in point is when proponents of the system maintain that it was instigated by fully democratic countries, and therefore is completely in order. Another argument along the same lines is that supranationality in reality contributes to maintaining democratic stability in the member states. 'In fact, it is this good effect which in practice decides the confidence of public opinion in the Union as a historical project.' Sverker Gustavsson argues that the key question is whether the working methods are democratic, not if they are legitimate. Neither cause nor effect is of any relevance to this question, according to Gustavsson.[20] One important question is whether the EU should be democratized by being assigned a supranational powerbase of its own, and by creating possibilities for citizens to demand political responsibility from legislators at the supranational level, for example, by assigning legislative powers to the European parliament. Another important

Figure 9.1   Supranational power and ideology

		Stronger supranational government	
		YES	NO
Supranational	YES	*Federalism*	*Legal liberalism*
powerbase	NO	*Functionalism*	*Gaullism*

question is whether supranationality should be taken further than at present. When those four issues are combined with the options 'yes' and 'no', four fields emerge as shown in Figure 9.1.

Division, according to this figure, will lead to four ideological theories – that is, federalism, functionalism, legal liberalism and Gaullism.[21] Based on Gustavsson's arguments, these can briefly be described as follows:

Legal liberalism allows maximum impact of market forces. Supranationality will be limited to the safeguarding of market rules within the Union. To achieve this, a new constitutional treaty is required, thus a supranationality that allows a minimum interference from both the European and national level.

Federalism in this context advocates the introduction of a two-chamber system including a distribution between the principles of 'one state – one vote' and 'one individual – one vote'. Supranationality should be used to pursue projects that are ideologically based to achieve, for example, full employment, regional balance, social citizenship etc.

Gaullism here involves defending formal independence of the member states, only accepting minor transfers of power to the supranational level. Arguments about formal and real power are rejected. The point of departure is that power accumulated at the supranational level is correspondingly lost at the national level. (The term Gaullism signifies an attachment to EU core areas. Precisely the same points of view on European co-operation could be used for desribing the EU sceptics in the smaller member states.)

Functionalism in this context concentrates on the functions of the Union, that is, on what can be seen as a practical decisionmaking process and, above all, the achieved results. The EU is considered as a purely unique structure and, therefore, cannot be assessed on the basis of traditional democratic criteria. The fact that EU institutions can decide through supranational authority, without having to answer for their exercise of power in general elections, means that they can make decisions in the interest of all. Neither have leaders of individual nations to answer in front of their voters, since decisions made are the results of secret compromises. This proceeding has therefore contributed to 'save' rather than 'undermine' real possibilities of the member states to achieve national self-determination. Otherwise, goes the argument, the member states would not have been able to establish post-war welfare states and democracies. Thus, functionalists do not wish to see any democratization that would enforce account-ability upon a supranational European government. Tasks must be performed and success is dependent rather on the absence than the presence of a democratic order at the European level.

It is evident from the preceding paragraph that the advantage for an ardent functionalist, is exactly the disadvantage for the ardent Gaullist; that is, if the countries do not submit to the prin-ciple of qualified majority at the European level, there will be no supranationality. Functionalists do not wish to have a federation, since, according to democratic principles, that requires that those in power can be removed. Instead, the current decisionmaking process is taken as a point of departure to enforce the greatest pos-sible integration, that is, optimizing the degree of supranationality and reducing the right of veto, but without democratization and parliamentarism.

For legal liberalists and federalists, on the other hand, parliament-arism at the European level is exactly what is sought, even though for different reasons. Sverker Gustavsson conceives that as entirely unrealistic, since it would assume the occurrence of a constitutional new start; that all member states simultaneously will happen to find themselves in an almost revolutionary situation, and agree to a new common constitution with this purport. He concludes that if you wish to increase supranationality, you have to give up democratic accountability at the national level. On the other hand, if you wish to retain democratic accountability, your have to give up aspirations for supranationality.[22]

Another characterization, which borders on the same problem complex has been made by Liesbet Hooghe and Gary Marks, Belgian and American political scientists respectively, on the basis of the situation during the last few decades. Following the collapse of national Keynesianism, when economic stagnation occurred and international competitiveness was reduced, EC co-operation was reorganized. The most important issues were, then, on the one hand, how political decisionmaking power and political participation were to be arranged, and on the other, where to draw the line of political influence on the economy. The major conflict is perceived to take part between the neoliberal aim, through the internal market, to protect the economy against political interference, and the middle and left-wing groups' ambition to harness the economy through a regulated capitalism. This opposite relationship may be illustrated by the two-dimensional Figure 9.2.

Besides the traditional left-right dimension, there is, in the European context, the common opposite dimension of supranationality contra nationalism. Consensus in this situation cannot be reached, according to Hooghe and Marks, as the EU evolves in a permanent conflict between different interests and ideologies, which manifest themselves in competing opinions about the political order in Europe. They do not maintain that will, with any certainty, entail the continuation of political integration. 'To understand European integration one has to recognize its *political* character, and analyze the struggle between governments, supranational actors and national and transnational interests.'[23]

Figure 9.2   Politics and supranationality versus nationalism I

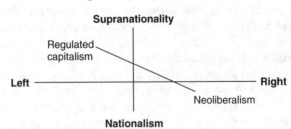

Comment

Even the above interpretations seem to perceive the problems as too general, that is, as if those political scientists coolly assume that the situation is largely the same always and everywhere. The historical factor, that is that the member countries have different historical heritages and conceptions of history, is hardly given any attention. However, that is not actually Sverker Gustavsson's intention, since he discusses general problems of democracy. His point, based on normatively confirmed democratic standpoints, is precisely that special circumstances or highly valued purposes can never legitimize a complete and fundamental deviation from democratic decision-making principles. The historical differences between countries substantiate the conclusion made by Gustavsson, since the democratic deficit is of varying importance for the political life of the member states, partly due to political cultural differences, and partly due to differences in size.

Clearly it is likely that there is significant variation between representatives of legal liberalism, federalism, Gaullism and functionalism. It is true that they are represented in party groups in the European parliament, but the different parties also have a national home base. What is described as 'Gaullism' may be an imperialistic position including advocates of a national 'Big Brother' perspective; however, it may also be true of the ambition of a small state to mark its independence. Foundations of national perspectives vary a great deal because of historical and geographical factors. The same position may be argued for on the basis of different perspectives. Functionalists may be those who find it useful to implement homogenizing decisions, on the basis of a large country perspective, as well as those employed by EU institutions. Therefore, their positions may well spring from completely different perspectives of interest.

The explanatory model formulated by Hooghe and Marks, according to the above figure, could probably be correspondingly interpreted. Evidently, their point of departure is the continental EU, where Christian Democrats and Social Democrats, although with certain differences, try to achieve a regulated capitalism. The opposite, according to their line of thought, is a British conservative with neo-liberal views, that is, a representative of Thatcherism. Therefore, it is logical to place neoliberalism in the field between 'Right' and 'Nationalism'. However, if the neoliberal lives in a country where his ideology has no chance to gain a political impact, the position in the figure will be entirely different. In countries with proportional representation, it is highly improbable that neoliberal political groupings will achieve parliamentary majority, and so be able to reshape society. However, here the EU offers an alternative. If, as a result of EU decisions, the purposes of legal liberalists can be achieved, it follows that it will be possible indirectly to enforce a policy in their own country for which it is impossible to obtain the required electoral support. In this case, neoliberalism has to be positioned in the field between 'Right' and 'Supranationality' (see Figure 9.3). However, there are elements within Scandinavian Social Democracy that are negative or sceptical to supranationality. Of course, some sort of regulated capitalism is desired, but not through increased supranationality, which people from a small country perspective do not feel able to influence to any significant extent. Instead of the position between 'Left' and 'Supranationality', it is the field between 'Left' and 'Nationalism' that is of immediate interest. The Scandinavian green parties, the left and centre parties will end up in the same field. However, they would prefer not to be classified as in favour of 'Nationalism' as opposed to 'Supranationality', but rather 'National independence'.

To conclude, the explanatory model and Figure 9.2 do not match when different cases are chosen than those suggested by Hooghe and Marks. The model may be valid for the EU core areas and for the United Kingdom, but definitely not for the EU as a whole. The difference between the member states' historical heritages and political cultures calls for a modification of the model, according to Figure 9.3.

Figure 9.3   Politics and supranationality versus nationalism II

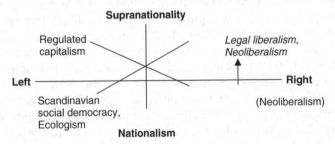

To summarize, it can be noted that research on European integration mainly follows two principal lines concerning the political process; one that emphasizes the emergence of a supra-state with its own ambitions, and one that emphasizes the interests of the member states in co-operating in order to strengthen themselves. However, it might also be argued that certain member states, the larger states, may wish to reinforce the supra-state with a view to gaining greater influence.

An interpretation of the political purpose

The purposes of the EU and the EMU

People today, almost without exception, welcome international understanding and international co-operation. Even though there will always be a few isolationists or eremites, it is no longer possible to imagine any other future than that of frequent contacts and inter-action between peoples and countries. Individual, geographical and socially and culturally conditioned differences will also remain in the future, but in the wider perspective, it is difficult to foresee any other kind of development than that of an international give-and-take in all areas of operation. International co-operative organizations and institutions are innumerable and are found in all human fields of activity. It is reasonable that any assessment of the European Union (EU) and its present and future functions must be made in the light of global, regional as well as local co-operation and rivalries. Therefore, it is natural that the EU may be conceived differently, depending on by whom and which parts of EU operations are being considered.

EU development, from the very first initiatives in the formation of the Coal and Steel Community to the present-day extensively developed Union, has progressed rapidly, considering that its members are nation states. What the final result of this development will be is a matter of widely differing opinions. There is, obviously, among some political parties, both in the national parliaments and in the European parliament, a clearly discernible ambition to develop EU further into a federal union. The EU Commission, in its documents, consistently emphasizes the ambition to strengthen the European identity, 'the shift to a more genuinely political Union' etc.[24] At the same time, it is quite obvious that none of the member states seek a European equivalent to the USA. However, it is not at all clear where the limit of an increased supranationality will be drawn. It may be relevant to ask whether the EU will be able to function as a mutual co-operation project if supranationality is taken any further than it is today.

Then, what is the real aim of the EU? The EU Information Centre of the *Riksdag* points out the following historical context:

> At the end of the Second World War, the continent of Europe lay in ruins. The idea of close and permanent cooperation between the war-weary nations of Europe was born out of a desire to secure peace and build economic prosperity.[25]

This was the reason why, in 1950, the proposal for what was to become the Coal and Steel Community was presented. The proposal aimed 'to establish a joint mechanism for controlling the industries that were at the very core of military armament, making a new war between the participating states unlikely'.[26] Thus, aspirations to promote both peace and prosperity are emphasized as the aim of what was to become the EU.

In historical retrospect, the European parliament presents the following aims of the first treaties: 'The avowed intentions of the founders of the ECSC were that it should be merely a first stage towards a "European Federation".'[27] The common market in coal and steel should make it possible to create a constitution that would also gradually extend into other areas, including the economic area, and eventually culminate in a politically unified Europe. 'The aim of the European Economic Community was to establish a common market based on the four freedoms of movement of goods, persons, capital and services and the gradual convergence of economic policies.'[28] The preambles of the three treaties show, according to the European Union, that the inspiration behind the creation of the Communities was the same, namely, the conviction that 'the states of Europe must work together to build a common future as this alone will enable them to control their destiny'.[29]

It would not be controversial to claim that the European parliament has persistently maintained federalist standpoints, while at the same time both the governments of the member states and the European

Commission, even if due to different reasons, have expressed more cautious views or rejected the idea of a federation.

The proposal of the Convention, submitted in June 2003, states that an aim of the Union is 'to promote peace, its values and the well-being of its peoples', but also free competition, a social market economy, solidarity, equality between men and women etc. However, is the EU needed for the achievement of this, or must the organization be assigned suitable objectives since the EU already exists? The Convention also states in terms of a compromise: 'These objectives shall be pursued by appropriate means, depending on the extent to which the relevant competences are attributed to the Union in the Constitution.'[30]

The aim of peace is perhaps most often referred to, namely that the ultimate purpose of the EU is the establishment of peace in this war-ridden continent. The high and good purpose is emphasized as such a highly desirable objective that all objections may be considered as petty or irrelevant: 'After all, this is a peace project.'

Concerning the EMU, it might not be considered controversial to maintain that this is *an economic project with a political intent, namely through a common monetary policy and currency to tighten the ties between the member states in mutual interdependence.* This is frequently debated in recently published literature on the EMU. A case in point is the description by the economists Martin Ådahl and Jörgen Eklund:

> The political principle behind the EU is the same as that which has been seen throughout the history of the EEC and later the EU: closer economic ties will lead to a stronger political integration, which is intended to bring peace and prosperity to the European continent...However, the EMU goes further. With the exception of the common Court of Justice, the EMU is obviously one of the most clearly stated supranational projects within the EU. Decisions on monetary policy are taken entirely by the common management of the ECB, without any negotiations between the nation states. Add the deeply rooted concept of national currencies and it is not difficult to understand why the most ardent EU advocates hope – and the most ardent adversaries fear – that the EMU is also the beginning of a federal state.[31]

The debate about the EMU has to a lesser degree concerned its economic effects, although there are widely differing assessments, and to a higher degree concerned whether the political implications are desirable or not. Moreover, opinions differ as to what these implications are, and how much of national decisionmaking competence will be transferred to the supranational level through the EMU, not least in the long-term perspective. Then how can one explain why the EMU was introduced at all and incorporated in the Maastricht Treaty? The following is a tentative interpretation along historical lines.

An interpretation based on the theories on modern Europe

The EU and its preceding institutions have existed for half a century, during which time the world has changed profoundly. The Cold War and the polarized East–West conflict have, after decades of balance of terror, been brought to an end by the collapse of the Soviet Union and the democratization of the East-European countries. The relinquishing of European empires in Asia and Africa; the entire North–South problem complex; the conflict in the Middle East; the emergence of new industrial nations and economic centres; and globalization in its widest sense, are other highly important factors, which have no doubt influenced development within the EU and its predecessors. Obviously, the EU, therefore, cannot be considered as existing independently of the rest of the world, nor of the historical heritage, which all its member states have carried and still carry.

The above-mentioned theories on the successful integration of Western Europe all take a point of departure in the countries' gradually increased prosperity, and the fact that this has taken place peacefully and in mutual interest. All member countries have gained a benefit and thus has the Union survived, even after the inclusion of even more member countries. However, this process has brought increasing integration. Therefore no one knows whether an even deeper integration that cannot be influenced by single member states, including, for example, supranational fiscal powers, will result in the breaking up of co-operation in a series of deep conflicts of interest. Such conflicts could, in principle, threaten the existence of the entire project. Federalists do not think so, and hope that the EU will become the European equivalent of the USA. Compared to the USA, the differences are, however, paramount and that is why that perspective cannot be considered as realistic. Rather it can be seen as a political-dogmatic theoretical construction, where the desire to adapt the terrain to the map is assumed to be enough for this to happen. Thus, the unconditional federalist support for the EMU project. The fact that legal liberalists, who wish increased supranationality in a few limited areas, support the EMU appears to be less logical. If those areas were limited to the guarantee of the free market and exclude economic control, for example common fiscal policy, it would be logical. However, should the EMU in the long-term perspective bring about a supranational order, entailing what legal liberalists least of all would wish, then the EMU would be most counterproductive. Finally, Gaullists should of course shun the EMU, according to the above description of their views. Yet, here the paradox emerges that the EMU can be seen as more or less enforced for Gaullist reasons. The context will be explained below.

The EMU may instead result in a centralization, conforming very well with traditional nation-state policies, although only considering some of the member states. It could even be maintained that the enforcement of the project has been accomplished by one member state in particular, that is France. However, the explanation is in line with the customary arguments, as presented above. Yet, there are other arguments, which might be considered stronger and more applicable to the self-image of Gaullist France and its role in world politics.

Was the EU originally founded with the aim of creating peace and prosperity? Maybe to some extent; however, the Cold War was, without doubt, a strong contributory factor, as was the need to mobilize the West-European countries against the Soviet threat. The structure and supranational decisionmaking system of the Coal and Steel Community were rational instruments to demolish the mistrust caused by old antagonisms. Thus, there were good reasons for all parties involved to accept this structure, since it was a way to strengthen the economy through co-operation. Moreover, for West Germany and Italy this was a way to become accepted by their former enemies, thereby acting as what has been shown by numerous researchers to be a kind of adjustment and reinforcement of the nation state to the actual situation. However, one party is often overlooked in this context, namely France.

Ever since the formation of the French state, its recurring ambition has been to extend borders to the north and east. Louis XIV and Napoleon are the most obvious exponents of this policy. The French aspirations to become a great power created a gigantic empire. The defeat by Prussia in 1871 was therefore an ignominy. The severe peace terms enforced upon Germany after World War I were largely a result of the French desire to humiliate Germany. The result is only too well known. Hitler's revanchist war and the rapid fall of France in spring 1940, the following years of occupation and the Vichy government punctured the French self-esteem. During the Fourth Republic, France sought to regain its self-esteem and international status by re-establishing its empire. However, these aspirations failed in Indochina, and its African colonies were relinquished following the struggle for Algeria, which also forced France to retreat. De Gaulle's assumption of power in 1958 and the establishment of the Fifth Republic signified the restoration of a strong French central power. The arena, in which France sought to recreate its honour and international influence was that of Western Europe. As the leading country in the EEC, France regained influence to compensate for the loss of its empire, and within an area where France, traditionally and in different ways, had sought to dominate and influence.

Gaullist EEC dominance meant that entrance applications of the United Kingdom were turned down twice. Only after de Gaulle lost power was Britain admitted and the customs union EEC became the EC. During this period, the so-called German miracle occurred; the remarkable economic growth of West Germany in combination with political democracy and stability. A significant basis for the West German economic growth was the Deutschmark and the priority given to low inflation by the *Bundesbank*. West Germany maintained a low international profile during this time, and developed into the greatest contributor of net payments within the customs union. By virtue of its strong economy, West Germany was able to increase its real influence within the EEC/EC. At the same time, France's need to maintain co-operation between both countries increased. The corresponding economic growth of Japan, and its rise to an international economic great power changed conditions for the EC. 'Europe' was to start competing with America as well as Japan, and, to some extent, with Russia, economically as well as politically, in order to play a more important international role. In the mid-1980s, work was initiated within the EC to standardize the economic regulatory framework, at the same time as the changes taking place within the

Soviet Union became apparent. The end of the Cold War, together with German reunification, changed the conditions for the EC. The response was the Maastricht Treaty for further integration and, in particular, the introduction of the EMU.

Why was the decision taken to establish the EMU? Most researchers point to the fact that these ideas had existed already in the early 1950s. However, that can hardly be a reasonable explanation, since, as a rule, all ideas have predecessors in other times and contexts. What was of decisive importance can most probably be found in the new situation brought about by the end of the Cold War, not the dissolution of the Soviet bloc, but the reunification of Germany. Germany thus became significantly larger than France, and could have been able to refer to the EC treaty, stipulating that the degree of influence should be determined by population. The democratization of Eastern Europe and the possibility that several East-European countries could become members of the EC, would definitely change the balance of power within the organization to the disadvantage of France. Germany was larger, had a stronger economy and could count on benefiting more than France, both economically and politically, from the affiliation of its eastern neighbours. For the French President François Mitterrand, nominally a socialist, but in reality an upholder of the traditional interests of the French nation state, the situation became acute, when, in 1990, the Soviet Union recognized the German reunification. The EMU became an opportunity for the French to get a share of the German economic power. For the German Federal Chancellor Kohl, the EMU was an instrument to make the other EC member states accept the German reunion and consequently a larger and stronger Germany in the heart of Europe. Thus, it was the national interests of the dominating EC countries, together with their mutual interdependence and wish to secure support, which resulted in the EMU, not any belief that the economy would improve. Part of the solution was that the *Bundesbank*, resisting until the end, was forced to comply; yet, the German condition was that the new central bank should be politically independent and give priority to low interest rates. Moreover, the European Central Bank (ECB) was located in Germany.

The negotiated compromises can be found in the Maastricht Treaty, but numerous practical problems remained when the EC through this process became the EU. For the EMU, convergence criteria were determined; however, the political dimension of this project was so powerful that when things came to the point, a blind eye was turned to the fulfilment of the conditions. In order to secure the political project, all candidates except Greece were approved, in spite of the fact that only the smallest nation, Luxembourg, clearly fulfilled the conditions. The forthcoming enlargement with the East gave rise to differing opinions as regards the use of the financial resources of the EU. The net beneficiary countries, above all the Mediterranean countries and Ireland, were worried that poorer countries would take part in the partition of the cake, and the net contributors, particularly Germany and later Sweden, had no interest in contributing more money. Moreover, no one wished to lose influence. The resulting compromise was the Treaty of Nice.

A few years after the introduction of the common currency, some effects may be discerned. One of these could be that the Mediterranean countries have become more disciplined in keeping their budgets, and maintaining a lower rate of inflation. However, at the time of writing, it does not seem probable that either France or Germany will be able to fulfil the demands of the convergence criteria, that is the budget terms and conditions that the EMU countries may not diverge from without being penalized. The rigidity of these conditions has been criticized by several continental politicians, and the Chairman of the European Commission, Romano Prodi, has even described them as 'stupid'.

The EU is a political project, based on large countries having more influence than small ones, and the treaties are interpreted accordingly. If all the rules and regulations were equally applicable to all member states, the Maastricht Treaty would not have been ratified, as Denmark voted against it. The same is true of the Treaty of Nice, since Ireland opposed that. The more increase there is in supranationality, the more difficult it becomes for small member states to maintain democratic control of the government of their own countries.

Summarizing the situation after the ratification of the Treaty of Nice, and the presentation of the proposal of the Convention in 2003, it can be established that France emerges as the easy winner. After the Treaty of Nice came into force, it may be noted that the structure of the EU, and the weighted influence of the member states based on their populations, have largely remained the same, despite the fact that Germany today is significantly larger than Italy, France and the United Kingdom. There are reasons to dispute the characterization of Gaullists as those who defend the rights of the nation state to determine in its own affairs. Rather, it may be maintained that French Gaullist pragmatism, partly through a socialist president, has succeeded in maintaining a disproportionate French influence in the EU. The original structure with a characteristically French administration has remained, as has the fact that the French language still is one of the EU administrative languages, although the Union has by far more German-speaking people. The Common Agricultural Policy, devouring half of the common resources along the lines of a planned economy, to a large extent provides the maintenance of the French agriculture; no major decisions are taken against the will of France. At the meeting of the European Council in Greece, in June 2003, France blocked all initiatives aimed at changing the Common Agricultural Policy. In short, the EU and its predecessors are primarily a French design, which, apart from official declarations, have in many respects served the purpose of using all possible means to enlarge, or at least maintain, French political world influence, particularly in Europe. Therefore the decision on the EMU was enforced in 1991–2, and the difficulties in breaking up compromises means that, ten years later, the decision is still maintained, in spite of the fact that the economic and other political circumstances have changed significantly.

Closing remarks

The establishment of the EU may be seen as a result of the beginning of the Cold War, and the establishment of the EMU as a result of the end of the Cold War. The EU has changed as the world and Europe have changed. For its members the organization has acted as an arena for negotiations and compromises; however, one in which the actors differ significantly. The EMU involves the establishment of a higher degree of supranationality, and the divergent influences on decisions made within the Union entail quite different outcomes of the supranationality. If all members refrain from the same kind of decisionmaking rights, this, in effect, will mean that the small members lose and the large ones win. Denmark, Sweden and other small countries cannot realistically count on anything else than submission to decisions taken by the larger countries. Supranationality for the larger countries appears less dramatic, as they, with their greater influence on the common decisionmaking process, may regain and even enlarge their influence. However, supranationality might strike back even on large countries. The eagerness to enclose the EMU decision in supranational inaccessibility, seems to have contributed to the fact that not even Germany can take decisions about its own economy, which could hardly have been foreseen by the German decisionmakers when they tied their economy to the EMU and its regulatory framework.

Maintenance of peace is often presented as an argument for increasing supranationality, and thereby also for the EMU. Certainly no wars have arisen among the member states, and since the early 1950s they have all been transformed into social welfare democracies, while also maintaining their national characters. Does that mean that the EU has successfully guaranteed lasting peace in Europe? The opinion of the European Commission is 'the obvious – but sometimes forgotten – fact that the most striking success of the European venture has been the peace and prosperity it has generated'.[32] That statement is also often found among the research community, although it is quite impossible to substantiate, simply because it is not true. The Nordic countries, which have not been in union with each other for a long time, illustrate the opposite, namely that supranationality is not a precondition for the creation of peace and prosperity. However, democracy appears to be an absolutely necessary element.

Within the next few years, when there will be nearly 30 member states, the EU will face some alternatives: *either* to firmly commit to an increasingly uniform and centralized structure, where the periphery will have a subsiding influence, and where conflicts of interests will become even deeper; *or* to develop a pluralistic and decentralized structure, allowing for different member states to co-operate in different ways in different issues. One scenario of the future EU might be to guarantee member states democratic rights of determination concerning their own affairs, and allowing for those countries that wish to deepen integration in certain areas, differently for the diverse EU regions. Those members who feel a considerably higher degree of affinity and conformity could, for example, continue the EMU project, whereas others may refrain from doing so. Such regions could be, for example the Nordic countries, the Balkans, Central

Europe etc., depending on which common issues the countries wish to co-operate in. A pluralistic, decentralized and regionalized EU could, if that was the case, become an important tool to integrate other European countries in mutually respectful and non-conformist co-operation, including such key countries as Turkey and Russia. An EU, progressing into the future with such ambitions, will always be prepared to adjust to changing circumstances, and might develop into a real pan-European peace project.

Notes

1. *http://www.riksdagen.se/eu/teman/nice/index.asp*, retrieved June 2003. The definition of qualified majority will be adjusted following the entrance of each new member state, so that the percentage of required votes will be between 71.26 and 73.4 per cent. When there are 27 member states, the minimum required votes for these decisions would be 255 out of a possible 345, that is 73.91 per cent.
2. The *Riksdag*, Minutes and Appendices: 2000/2001: KUU1.
3. D. Mitrany, *A Working Peace System*, London: Oxford University Press, 1943.
4. The US demanded European co-operation as a requisite for Marshall Aid in 1947, and the following year saw the formation of the OEEC, the predecessor of the OECD. A brief background of the idea of a European community can be found in, for example, J. Torbacke, 'Från dröm till verklighet – Europatankens historia', *Aktuellt om historia*, 1, 1995.
5. K. Deutsch, *Political Community and the North Atlantic Area*, Princeton, NJ: Princeton University Press 1957.
6. For neofunctionalist writings, see, for example, E.B. Haas, *The Uniting of Europe: Political, Social and Economic Forces, 1950–1957*, London: Stevens, 1958; and E.B. Haas, *Beyond the Nation State: Functionalism and International Organization*, Stanford, CA: Stanford University Press, 1964; L. Lindberg, *The Political Dynamics of European Economic Integration*, Stanford, CA: Stanford University Press, 1963; R.O. Koehane and J.S. Nye, 'International Interdependence and Integration', in F. Greenstein and N. Polsby Jr (eds), *Handbook of Political Science, vol. 8, International Politics*, Reading, MA: Addison Wesley, 1975. See also M. af Malmborg, *Den ståndaktiga nationalstaten: Sverige och den västeuropeiska integrationen 1945–1959*, Lund: Lund University Press, 1994, pp. 13–16.
7. R. Aron, 'Old Nations, New Europe', in S.R. Graubard (ed.), *A New Europe?*, Boston: Oldbourne, 1964, p. 50.
8. See for example S. Hoffman, 'Obstinate or Obsolete? The Fate of the Nation-State and the Case of Western Europe', *Daedalus. Journal of the American Academy of Arts and Sciences*, 2, 1996.
9. For example A.S. Milward, *The Reconstruction of Western Europe 1945–51*, London: Methuen, 1984; and A.S. Milward, *The European Rescue of the Nation-State*, London: Routledge, 1992.

168   *National Policy in Disguise*

10. A.S. Milward, 'The Frontier of National Sovereignity', in S. Gustavsson and L. Lewin (eds), *The Future of the Nation-State: Essays on cultural pluralism and political integration*, London, New York: Routledge, 1996.
11. Hofstede has published a number of studies on international management, for example, G. Hofstede, *Cultures and Organizations: Software of the Mind*, London: McGraw-Hill, 1991. His conclusions can be found in G. Hofstede, 'The Nation-State as a Source of Common Mental Programming: Similarities and Differences Across Eastern and Western Europe', Gustavsson and Lewin, *The Future of the Nation-State*.
12. M. Jachtenfuchs and B. Kohler-Koch (eds), *Europäische Integration*, Opladen: Leske and Budrich, 1996; B. Kohler-Koch, 'Die Welt regieren ohne Weltregierung', in C. Böhret and G. Wewer (eds), *Regieren im 21. Jahrhundert – zwischen Globalisierung und Regionalisierung*, Opladen: Leske und Budrich, 1993, pp. 109–41. See also R.O. Koehane and S. Hoffman, 'Institutional Change in Europe in the 1980s', in R.O. Koehane and S. Hoffman (eds), *The New European Community. Decisionmaking and Institutional Change*, Oxford: Westview Press, 1991, pp. 1–39.
13. P.C. Schmitter (ed.), *Experimenting with Scale in Western Europe*, New York: Cambridge University Press, 1997. See also L. Parri, 'Territorial Political Exchange in Federal and Unitary Countries', *West European Politics*, 12, 1989, pp. 197–219.
14. K. Goldmann, *Övernationella idéer: EU som ideologiskt projekt*, Stockholm: SNS, 2003, p. 155.
15. *Ibid.*, p. 155.
16. *Ibid.*, p. 156.
17. *Ibid.*, p. 158.
18. 'The Schuman Declaration', D. de Giustiano (ed.), *A Reader in European Integration*, London: Longman, 1996.
19. An account and discussion of the Schuman Declaration and Monnet's memo can be found in Gustavsson, S. 'Varför överstat utan demokrati', in U. Bernitz, S. Gustavsson and L. Oxelheim (eds), *Europaperspektiv 1998*, Stockholm: Santérus, 1998, pp. 92–9.
20. S. Gustavsson, 'Ett demokratiskt Europa', in U. Wallin, (ed.), *En nykter 75:a: Om politik, nykterhet och samhälle*, Stockholm: Sober, 1996, pp. 18ff.
21. *Ibid.* pp. 24ff. Sverker Gustavsson uses the traditional term 'Gaullism' although in this context it would preferably be substituted with another term.
22. *Ibid.*, pp. 38ff.
23. L. Hooghe, and G. Marks, 'Hur motsättningar skapar gemenskap', in Bernitz, Gustavsson and Oxelheim *Europaperspektiv 1998*.
24. These standpoints can be found in numerous EU documents, for example, *Regeringskonferensen (IGC) 1996: Kommissionens yttrande (Commission Opinion)*, 1996.
25. 'The Origins and Development of the EU, Fact sheet no. 1', *The EU Information Centre*, The *Riksdag*, August 2002.
26. Ibid.
27. Ibid.

28. Ibid.
29. *http://www.europarl.eu.int/factsheets/1.1.1.sv.htm*, retrieved 8 June 2003.
30. *http://european.convention.eu.int/docs/Treaty/cv00820-re01.sv03.pdf*, retrieved 5 July 2003.
31. M. Ådahl and J. Eklund, *Allt om EMU*, Stockholm: SNS, 2003, pp. 160f.
32. *Regeringskonferensen (IGC) 1996: Kommissionens yttrande (Commission Opinion)* (1996), p. 23.

Index